# On a Life Well Spent

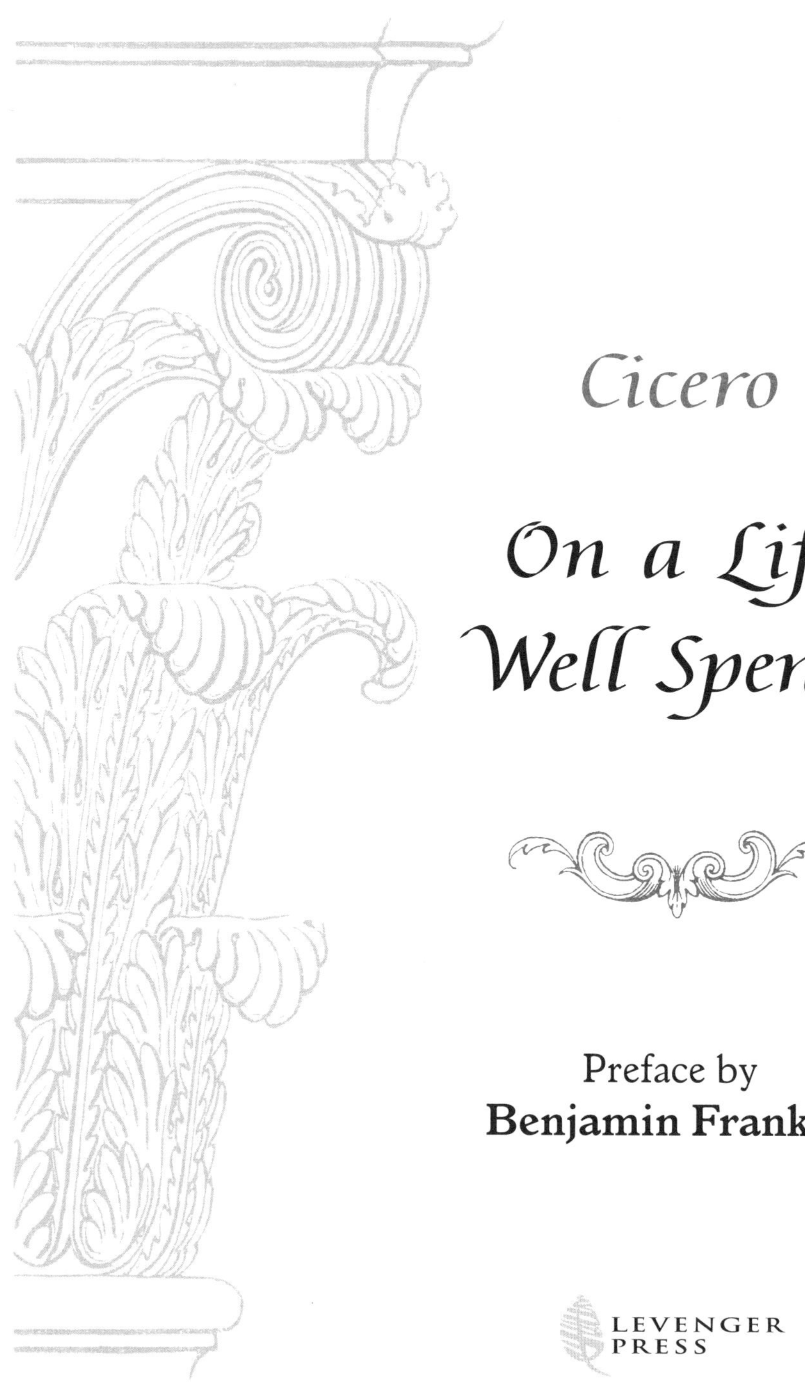

Cicero

# On a Life Well Spent

Preface by
**Benjamin Franklin**

LEVENGER PRESS

Published by Levenger Press
420 South Congress Avenue
Delray Beach, Florida 33445 USA
800.544.0880
Levengerpress.com



From the work originally printed in 1744 by Benjamin Franklin, with explanatory notes by James Logan, and titled *M. T. Cicero's Cato Major or His Discourse of Old-Age.*

First and second impressions, 2006
Third impression, 2007

The Library of Congress has cataloged the hardcover edition as follows:

Cicero, Marcus Tullius.
[Cato maior de senectute. English]
On a life well spent / Cicero ; preface by Benjamin Franklin.
p. cm.
"From the edition originally printed in 1744 by Benjamin Franklin, with explanatory notes by James Logan, and titled M.T. Cicero's Cato major or his Discourse of old-age"--T.p. verso.
Includes bibliographical references.
ISBN 1-929154-20-8 (hardcover)
1. Old age--Early works to 1800. 2. Conduct of life--Early works to 1800. I. Title.
PA6308.C2L6 2005
875'.01--dc22

2005005133

ISBN-13: 978-1-929154-23-4
ISBN-10: 1-929154-23-2

*Cover and book design by Danielle Furci*
*Mim Harrison, Editor*

# Contents

# Introduction

Marcus Tullius Cicero was born in 106 B.C. E. and murdered in 43 B.C. E. By the standard of the day, he was an old man when he died. And yet his accomplishments, both as a person of ideas and a man of action, were never hindered by his advancing years. As he affirms again and again in this work, thought and deed transcend the physical.

The Cicero of ancient Rome was a formidable politician, a successful lawyer, a powerful orator whose speeches to the Roman Senate would resound for centuries, and above all, a principled statesman. *Moralis,* a word he coined, was the forerunner of our *moral;* his Verrine Orations were a blistering attack on political corruption. Although he was a friend of Julius Caesar's, he refused to join political forces with him. His intractable allegiance to a republican form of government and an abhorrence of dictatorships would literally be the death of him: Mark Antony had him killed for it.

But while he may have been reviled in his time by his political adversaries, Cicero has been revered through the ages

as one of the greatest writers of antiquity. He had a gift for making the philosophical works of the Greeks accessible in his own language, and it is Cicero's Latin that has endured. He wrote poetry as an adolescent, volumes of letters throughout his life and *De Oratore* at the age of fifty-one.

But he really hit his stride as a writer when he reached his sixties.

That is when he produced his masterpiece on statecraft, *On the Republic,* advocating a constitution that combined elements of a monarchy, an oligarchy and a democracy. He also wrote a four-volume treatise on philosophical method, a five-volume "conversation" on the pursuit of happiness, the three-volume *Nature of the Gods,* as well as *Foretelling the Future, On Supreme Good and Evil, Destiny, Duties* and the work presented here, *De Senectute:* on aging.

In the 1700s the young American colonies were embracing the classical teachings of ancient Rome and Greece in what the scholar Meyer Reinhold called their quest for "useful knowledge." It was the Age of Enlightenment, when the importance of the individual and the concepts of happiness and freedom were shaping intellectuals' thought. (*Beatitudo,* another word that Cicero coined, is what we know as *happiness.*) So it was fitting that Cicero appealed to a group that was determined to install a republican form of government—the likes of Thomas Jefferson, John Adams and a Philadelphia printer named Benjamin Franklin.

Franklin (1706-1790), very much a man who embraced useful knowledge, had established himself as a printer in 1728 and started publishing his *Poor Richard's Almanack* four years later. In 1744 the thirty-eight-year-old Franklin printed a translation of Cicero's *De Senectute,* titling it M.T. CICERO'S *CATO MAJOR* OR HIS DISCOURSE OF OLD-AGE. It gave him much pleasure to publish this work; as the biographer Stacy Schiff observed, Cicero's overarching message of a life well lived would find its way into Franklin's own writings and pronouncements. And Franklin would certainly wear his own mantle of old age with relish.

James Logan (1674-1751), a fellow Philadelphian who was considered one of the most scholarly men in America, translated the work for Franklin's edition and provided copious explanatory footnotes. Franklin pronounced it the "first translation of a classic in this Western World"; it was in all probability the first printed in America.

Logan had been William Penn's secretary and had held important government posts in Pennsylvania. A man of science, letters and great wealth, he amassed a collection of books that totaled close to three thousand volumes. In 1731, when Franklin founded his subscription library, the Library Company of Philadelphia, he turned to Logan for advice on

which books he should carry. Franklin and Logan remained friends and admirers of one another for years.

And Cicero, however indirectly, became a guiding force in shaping the United States of America. Deeply embedded in the foundation of the Declaration of Independence and the Constitution are the tenets of republicanism that Cicero cherished and the three-branch system of government he championed.

John Adams was one of the founding fathers who revered the ancient's political wisdom, as David McCullough described in his biography of the second president: Adams read *De Senectute* again and again throughout his long and well-spent life. No doubt he found truth and solace in Cicero's observation that "a life employed in the pursuit of useful knowledge, in honourable actions and the practice of virtue" yielded "an unspeakable comfort to the soul."

Perhaps each age takes from Cicero what it values most. In the eighteenth century, his views on the merits of a republican form of government resonated strongly with the people shaping America's democracy. In the twenty-first century, his views on aging serve as enlightenment that age need not diminish a person's capacity for learning and doing. And so for this edition, a reprise of Franklin's 1744 landmark publication, we selected the title *On a Life Well Spent*.

We also elected to relocate Logan's one hundred and two footnotes to the back, as endnotes, where they can delight the interested reader. And while we have retained the spelling and punctuation of Franklin's original, we have set it in a modern font—minus the elongated *s*, and with apologies to the Philadelphia printer. Both these measures succeed, we hope, in making Cicero and his ageless wisdom more accessible to our age.

# Benjamin Franklin's Preface

## *The Printer to the Reader.*

This Version Of CICERO's Tract *de Senectute,* was made Ten Years since, by the Honourable and Learned Mr. LOGAN, of this City; undertaken partly for his own Amusement, (being then in his 60th Year, which is said to be nearly the Age of the Author when he wrote it) but principally for the Entertainment of a Neighbour then in his grand Climacteric; and the Notes were drawn up solely on that Neighbour's Account, who was not so well acquainted as himself with the Roman History and Language: Some other Friends, however, (among whom I had the Honour to be ranked) obtained Copies of it in M. S. And, as I believed it to be in itself equal at least, if not far preferable to any other Translation of the same Piece extant in our Language, besides the Advantage it has of so many valuable Notes, which at the same time they clear up the Text, are highly instructive and entertaining; I resolved to give it an Impression, being confident that the Publick would not unfavourably receive it.

A certain Freed-man of *Cicero*'s is reported to have said of a medicinal Well, discovered in his Time, wonderful for the Virtue of its Waters in restoring Sight to the Aged, *That it was a*

*Gift of the bountiful Gods to Men, to the end that all might now have the Pleasure of reading his Master's Works.* As that Well, if still in being, is at too great a Distance for our Use, I have, *Gentle Reader* as thou seest, printed this Piece of *Cicero*'s in a large and fair Character, that those who begin to think on the Subject of *OLD-AGE,* (which seldom happens till their Sight is somewhat impair'd by its Approaches) may not, in Reading, by the *Pain* small Letters give the Eyes, feel the *Pleasure* of the Mind in the least allayed.

I shall add to these few Lines my hearty Wish, that this first Translation of a *Classic* in this *Western World* may be followed with many others, performed with equal Judgment and Success; and be a happy Omen, that *Philadelphia* shall become the Seat of the *American* Muses.

Philadelphia, Febr. 29.

1743, 4

*The best Armour of Old Age is a well spent Life preceeding it; a Life employed in the Pursuit of useful Knowledge, in honourable Actions and the Practice of Virtue; in which he who labours to improve himself from his Youth, will in Age reap the happiest Fruits of them; not only because these never leave a Man, not even in the extreamest Old Age; but because a Conscience bearing Witness that our Life was well spent, together with the Remembrance of past good Actions, yields an unspeakable Comfort to the Soul.*

*SAY,* [1]Titus, *if some sovereign*
*Balm I find*
*To sooth your Cares, and calm*
*your ruffled Mind,*
*Shan't I deserve a Fee?*
For I may address you, Atticus, in the same Lines,
in which the [2]Poet,
*In Heart as great, as in his Fortunes poor,* applied to [3]Flaminius:
Tho' I am fully assured, you are far from being
in his Condition disturb'd with Thoughts,
*That wrung his Soul the live-long Nights and Days.*

For I well know the Evenness and just Composure of yours, and that you took not only your Name from Athens, but also brought home with you those nobler Improvements, the most consummate Prudence and Humanity. And yet, to be free with you, I cannot but think you are sometimes touched with the same Pains at Heart, that, I assure you, deeply affect me. [4]But these are Matters of a more important Weight, that require Arguments from a deeper Fund to support us under them; which may hereafter be applied to them.

THE SUBJECT I have now chose to write on, is OLD AGE; which, as it is advancing on us both, and in a little Time must unavoidably seize us, I would look out, and endeavour to find the best and surest Means, to make the Burthen of it sit as easy on us as possible. Tho' for your Part, I am well assured, that as you bear all Accidents and Events with the greatest Firmness and Moderation; so you will equally dispense with all the Inconveniencies that can attend this State. But as I resolved to write on the Subject, you (Atticus) of all Men appeared to me the most worthy and proper to direct it to; for being made yours, we may in common apply it to our Use together.

[5]And as to my own Part in it, I must own, the Thoughts that flowed on me from the Subject, in composing it, proved so entertaining and delightful to me, while about it, that they have not only divested the Prospect of Old Age, now before us, of every thing shocking or frightful, but they have rendred my Expectations of it even agreeable and comfortable.

Which leads me to say, We can never sufficiently admire the Excellency of Philosophy; to whose Dictates whoever submits,

*The Thoughts that flowed on me from the Subject proved so entertaining and delightful that they have not only divested the Prospect of Old Age of every thing shocking or frightful, but they have rendred my Expectations of it even agreeable and comfortable.*

he will never find himself at a Loss in any Stage or Condition of Life, to render it not only supportable, but easy: But on other Philosophical Subjects I have already wrote several Tracts and shall still continue to write. This on Old Age (as I have said) comes to you.

I choose for my Speaker in it not [6]Tithonus, as Aristo of Chio laid his; for a fabulous Person would take off from the Weight of it; but Old [7]Marcus Cato; that the Respect paid to his Name and Character, may give the greater Force and Authority to what is said. At his House I suppose [8]Scipio and Lælius to be met, expressing their Wonder to the Old-Man, how with such Ease and Chearfulness he could support the Weight of his Years; to which he fully answers them. And if his Language appear somewhat refined here, above what we meet with in his own Writings, I desire it may be attributed to his learning Greek, and reading their Authors; on which, 'tis well known, he spent much Time and Pains in his latter Days. In this Discourse however, you have my own Sentiments on the Subject, which I give you as follows; and thus they begin:

## II.

SCIPIO.

LÆLIUS HERE with me, Cato, as we greatly admire your Wisdom and vast Compass of Knowledge in general, so we have been particularly wondering to see how very easily and chearfully you bear your Age; for we can't perceive it gives you any Manner of Trouble; while we have observed others complaining of theirs, as if the Burthen were unsupportable.

CATO.

Indeed, my Friends, you place your Wonder on a Matter far below deserving it, a Business in which there is little or no Difficulty at all; provided proper Measures be taken in it. For know this, that those who have no Aid or Support within themselves, to render their Lives easy, will find every State irksome: While such as are convinced, they must owe their Happiness to themselves, and that if they cannot find it in their own Breasts, they will never meet with it from abroad; will never consider any thing as an Evil, that is but a necessary Effect of the established Order of Nature; which Old Age most undoubtedly is. 'Tis certainly strange, that while all Men hope they may live to attain it, any should find Fault with it, when it comes to their Share. Yet such is the Levity, Folly, and Perverseness of Mankind, that we see there is nothing more common.

But, oh! they say, it has crept on us too fast, and overtaken us sooner than we thought or expected. In the first Place, pray who put them on thinking wrong? How can they say, Old Age creeps faster on Manhood, than Manhood succeeded Youth and Childhood? Or how would it sit lighter at the Age of Eight Hundred Years, if that were the Term of it, than at Eighty? For the longer Duration of the preceeding Age, when once 'tis past, abates Nothing from the Effects of Old Age, when come; nor affords any Relief against the Follies and Weakness of such as sink under it. Wherefore, if you have, as you say, admired my Wisdom, (which I wish were equal to your Opinion of it, and that I truly merited the Name I bear) I know nothing it consists in more effectually than this, that I follow Nature, my most excellent Guide, as my God, and submit to his Power in all things; who if, thro' his Conduct, all the preceeding Parts of Life have been well performed, it is not probable, that he will suffer the last Act, as 'tis common with bad Poets, to wind up ill.

*How can they say, Old Age creeps faster on Manhood, than Manhood succeeded Youth and Childhood? Or how would it sit lighter at the Age of Eight Hundred Years than at Eighty?*

But it was absolutely necessary, that some Term, some Period should be set; and that, as it is with the Fruits of Trees, and of the Earth, Seasons should be allowed for their Springing, Growing, Ripening, and at last to drop. This wise Men will submit to, and chearfully bear: Nor could any thing else be

meant by the Stories told of the Giants Warring against the Gods, than Men's Rebelling against Nature and its Laws.

*As it is with the Fruits of Trees, and of the Earth, Seasons should be allowed for their Springing, Growing, Ripening, and at last to drop.*

LÆLIUS.

But, Cato, you would highly oblige us both (for I may venture to speak for Scipio as well as myself, since we both hope, or doubtless wish at least, to live to be old in our Turn) if you would be pleased to instruct us before-hand, how, and by what Methods, we may avoid the Inconveniencies that generally attend Old Age, so as to render it the more easy to us, when we reach it.

CATO.

With all my Heart, Lælius, in case you both desire it.

SCIPIO.

We both earnestly desire it, Cato, if not too troublesome; for as you are now well advanced towards the End of a long Journey, which we probably are to travel after you, we would gladly know of you, how you find it, in the Stage you are arrived at.

CATO.

WELL, I shall do my best to satisfy you. I have indeed been divers times in Company with other Old Men, my Equals, as you know the Proverb, *Birds of a Feather will flock together*; when they have been loud in their Complaints of the Inconveniencies of Old Age; particularly [9]Caius Salinator and Spurius Albinius, Men of Consular Dignity; who used heavily to lament, that they had out-liv'd all the Enjoyments in Life, for which it was worth the living; and that they found themselves slighted and forsaken by those who had formerly followed them, and had treated them with the highest Respect. But to me such Men appear to lay their Charge intirely wrong; for if what they complained of, were owing only to their Years, the Case must be the same with me, and all others of the like Age: Yet I have known several who have lived to be very old, without complaining at all; for they appeared not only easy, but pleased at their being delivered from the Tyranny of their former youthful Passions; and far from finding themselves slighted, were still honoured and revered by those about them.

But the true Ground of such Complaints lies wholly in the Manners of the Men: For such as take Care to be neither peevish, humoursome, nor passionate in Old Age, will find it tolerable enough; but a perverse Temper, a fretful or an inhumane Disposition, will, where ever they prevail, render any State of Life whatsoever unhappy.

LÆLIUS.

That is very true, Cato, but may not some alledge, it is your easy Circumstances in Life, with your Power and Dignity, that produce this happy Effect, and render your Old Age in particular so easy; but these, you know, are Articles that fall but to very few People's Share.

*I have known several who have lived to be very old, without complaining at all; for they appeared not only easy, but pleased at their being delivered from the Tyranny of their former youthful Passions.*

CATO.

I confess, Lælius, there may be something in what you say; but the Point lies not altogether there: For, as 'tis related of Themistocles, that a certain [10]Seriphian having on some Difference told him, that if he was great, it was owing to the Reputation of his Country, and not to himself: 'Tis true indeed, replied Themistocles; if I had been born in Seriphos, I should never have been great, nor would you, if you had been born an Athenian: So, much the same may be said of Old Age; for 'tis certain, that to one oppressed with Poverty, however otherwise qualified, Old Age can never prove easy; nor to a weak imprudent Person, however rich, can it be otherwise than troublesome.

*A perverse Temper, a fretful or an inhumane Disposition, will render any State of Life whatsoever unhappy.*

But the best Armour of Old Age, Scipio and Lælius, is a well spent Life preceeding it; a Life employed in the Pursuit of useful Knowledge, in honourable Actions and the Practice of Virtue; in which he who labours to improve himself from his Youth, will in Age reap the happiest Fruits of them; not only because these never leave a Man, not even in the extreamest Old Age; but because a Conscience bearing Witness that our Life was well spent, together with the Remembrance of past good Actions, yields an unspeakable Comfort to the Soul.

# IV.

WHEN I was a Youth, I took a strong Affection for [11]Quintus Maximus, who recovered Tarentum, tho' then well advanced in Years, as if he had been my Equal: For, there was in that Great Man, a solid Gravity, tempered with an engaging Sweetness; which in his Old Age did not at all alter or abate. Yet he was not very old, tho' somewhat stricken, when I first applied myself to him; for he was [12]the first time Consul but the Year after I was born, and in his fourth Consulate I was in the Service, tho' very [13]young, at Capua; the fifth Year after this I went Quæstor to Tarentum, then I was made Ædile, and [14]four Years after, Prætor, when Tuditanus and Cethegus were Consuls, and when Maximus, being then very old, [15]spoke for the [16]*Cincian* Law against Presents and Fees.

He was also far in Years when, continuing in Arms as if he had been in his Bloom, he commanded the Army against Annibal, and by his Patience and declining to fight, broke that General's Measures, tho' then in his Heat of Youth triumphing on his vast Successes. Which our Friend *Ennius* justly expresses in these Lines:

*One Man our State retriev'd by wise Delays;*
*For he of Blame regardless as of Praise,*
*His Country's Safety only had in View:*
*Wherefore his Fame still more illustrious grew,*
*And to the vaulted Skies on soaring Pinions flew.*

But how admirable was his Vigilance, his Skill and Contrivance in the Recovery of [17]Tarentum? Upon which I remember, Salinator, who, having lost the Town, had fled into the Castle, telling Fabius boastingly in my hearing, that if it had not been for him, he would not have gained Tarentum: 'Tis very true, replied Fabius, smiling, for if you had not lost it I should not have recover'd it. Nor did he excell in Arms more than in Civil Affairs; for when Consul the second time, his Collegue Spurius Servilius refusing to concern himself, he [18]resolutely opposed Caius Flaminius, the Tribune of the People, in his Attempt to divide amongst the Commons the Lands taken from the Piceni and Gauls. And tho' he was himself [19]Augur, he freely declared, that the best Auspices were always to act for the Good of the State, and the worst to act against it.

*He was far in Years when he commanded the Army against Annibal, and by his Patience and declining to fight, broke that General's Measures, tho' then in his Heat of Youth.*

Many were the Excellencies I observed in that Great Man; but none with more Wonder than his Behaviour on the Death of his Son Marcus, a Person of very great Merit, who had also been Consul. I have by me the Funeral Oration he composed and delivered himself at his [20]Funeral Pile; which as often as I look on, I can scarce think even the greatest of the Philosophers worthy to be compared to him.

Nor was he great in publick Life only; for he excelled yet more in private, and within his own Walls: How noble were his Discourses there! How instructive his Precepts! What a vast Knowledge of Antiquity was he possessed of! How skill'd in the Laws, and in Augury! For a Roman, he was very learned; and he had treasured up in his Memory, not only all the Wars of Rome, but those of other Nations. And I was on all Occasions no less fond of hearing him speak, than as I had been assured of what I then feared, and what has since accordingly proved too true; that when he was once taken from us, I should never find another Man to improve by.

*For a Roman, he was very learned; and he had treasured up in his Memory, not only all the Wars of Rome, but those of other Nations.*

## V.

BUT YOU may wonder, perhaps, that on this Occasion I should run so largely into the Praises of Fabius: 'Tis on this View only, that from this Account of him, you may be convinced, that it would be almost impious to imagine, the Old Age of a Person, who thus acted and behaved to the last, can be esteemed unhappy.

'Tis true, that all Men can't be Scipio's or Fabius's, to have the Pleasure of reflecting on such great Actions in their past Life, as their taking of Towns, or their Victories by Land or Sea, and their Triumphs for them. Nor is this at all necessary to Man's Happiness: For a calm contemplative Life, or a Life well and virtuously spent in the just Discharge of one's immediate Duty in any Station, will ever be attended with a Serenity of Mind in Old Age: Such a Life as we learn Plato led, who died at his Studies in the Eighty-first Year of his Age: Such as that of Isocrates, who is said to have wrote his Oration, called the [21]*Panathenaic,* in his Ninety-fourth Year, and to have lived Five Years after; whose Master, Gorgias of Leontium, lived One Hundred and Seven Years, and till his

Death never left off his Studies. This Man being asked, how at such an Age he could think Life desirable, answered, Because he had no Reason to complain of Life, nor did he feel any real Inconveniency from Age: An Answer truly noble, and worthy of a great and learned Soul.

*A calm contemplative Life, or a Life well and virtuously spent in the just Discharge of one's immediate Duty in any Station, will ever be attended with a Serenity of Mind.*

It is the Weak and Foolish only, who impute to Old Age what is purely owing to themselves. Ennius, whom I just now quoted, was far from this; for in these Lines,

*As the swift Racer, that has often run*
*Th' Olympic Course, and oft the Prize has won,*
*Rests quiet in Old-Age, when his fleet Labour's done;*

He compares his own Old Age to that of a noble Race-Horse, which after his Victories, was allowed to live at Ease. But you cannot but remember the Man himself; for now, under the late Consuls Titus Flaminius and Marcus Attilius, it is but Nineteen Years since his Death, which happen'd in the Consulate of Marcius Philippus the second time, and Servilus Cæpio; the same Year that I, then Sixty-five Years of Age, with a firm clear Voice, and full Strength Of [22]Sides, spoke for and carried the [23]*Voconian* Law. Ennius, then at the Age of Seventy Years (for so long he lived) bore those two heavy Loads, as most Men would account them, *viz.* Age and Poverty, in such a Manner, that he really appeared rather delighted, than to be at all uneasy under them.

# VI.

BUT ON considering the Subject we are upon, I find there are four Inconveniencies charged on Old Age, which, they say, render it unhappy. One is, that it disables Men from Business; another, that it renders the Body infirm; the third, that it deprives us of the Pleasures of Life; and lastly, that it is the next Neighbourhood to Death. Now let us examine the Weight of each of these particularly, and see how far the Complaint is just.

'Tis said, it disables from Business: But pray what kind of business? Is it such as Youth is capable of? And because Men have not still the same bodily Strength they had in Youth, are they therefore uncapable of what is properly the Business of Age? Did Fabius, think you, do nothing? Did your Father [24]Lucius Paulus, Scipio, my dear deceased Son's Father-in-Law, do nothing? Did the [25]Fabricius's, the [26]Curius's, the [27]Coruncanius's, and such other Old Men, do nothing, when by their Counsels and Authority they supported and steer'd the Common-wealth? [28]Appius Claudius was not only old, but had also the Misfortune to be blind; yet he, when the Senate seemed inclin'd to make a Peace, and enter into an Alliance with Pyrrhus, had Courage

enough to express himself to the Sense which Ennius gives us in his Annals in Verse:

*What Frenzy now has your wild Minds possest?*
*You, who were erst with sagest Counsels blest,*
*Your selves on sure Destruction thus to throw!*

With the rest that follows; spoke with great Strength and Gravity; for you know the Poem: But the Speech itself that Appius then made in the Senate, is still extant in his own Words. And this Part he acted no less than seventeen Years after he was the last time Consul, which was ten Years after the first: And before he was Consul the first time, he had been Censor. Which shews, that in the Time of Pyrrhus's War, he must have been very old; yet this Account of him we have from our Ancestors.

*They talk idly who pretend that Age disables from Business. They might with as much Justice assert, that a Pilot on board a Ship does nothing, because he neither mounts the Shrowds, hawls the Ropes, nor works at the Pump.*

They talk idly therefore, who pretend that Age disables from Business. They might with as much Justice assert, that a Pilot on board a Ship does nothing, because he neither mounts the Shrowds, hawls the Ropes, nor works at the Pump; but without any bodily Labour, minds only the Steerage, and directs the Helms-Man; which is of more Importance to the Ship's Preservation, than the Work of all the rest besides. For 'tis neither by bodily Strength, nor Swiftness, nor Agility, that momentous Affairs are carried on; but by Judgment, Counsel, and Authority: The Abilities for which are so far from failing in Old Age, that they truly increase with it.

*'Tis neither by bodily Strength, nor Swiftness, nor Agility, that momentous Affairs are carried on; but by Judgment, Counsel, and Authority.*

Unless you imagine that I, who, when I was in the several Stations of a Soldier, of Tribune, of Lieutenant General, and of Consul, personally active in the War, am now idle and do nothing, because I am no longer, as formerly, in the Field. But tho' not there, it will be allowed, I believe, that I am employed, at least, to full as good Purpose at home. I now direct in the Senate what our Armies are to do abroad, and lay down the Plan before-hand, how our dangerous Rival, Carthage, that I am sure has been long meditating further Mischief, is to be prevented in her Designs, and effectually humbled. For I shall ever think, while that Place stands, it will be contriving our Ruin; and that short of its total Destruction, Rome can never be secure. And the Glory of accomplishing this, [29]Scipio, I hope the immortal Gods have reserved for you; that what your excellent Grandfather made so great and happy a Progress in, may by your Virtue and Conduct, as his worthy Successor, be compleated.

This is now the thirty-third Year, since that Great Man was taken from us; but his glorious Actions will perpetuate his Fame for ever. He died the Year before I was Censor, nine Years after my Consulate, under which at the ensuing Election he was chosen again, and made the second time Consul. But had his Life been protracted to a Hundred Years, can you suppose it could ever have proved burthensome to him? He would not then indeed, as formerly, have given Proofs of his Abilities in youthful Exercises as Racing, Leaping, Tilting or Fencing; but

he would have done it abundantly by Strength of Reason, cool Judgment, and mature Counsel.

And hence it is, that because it has been constantly observed, that Old-Men principally excell in these, therefore our Ancestors gave the great Council of the State the Title of *Senate*, as consisting of a Body of *Senes*, or Old-Men, as the Word imports. The Lacedemonians also, for the same Reasons, give their supream Council no other Title than that of the *Old-Men*. And to shew the Justness of this, if you look into foreign Story, you will find, that the Downfall of the greatest States has been generally owing to the giddy Administration of unexperienced Young Men; as on the contrary, others have been supported, or the tottering have been recovered, by the Prudence and wise Counsels of the Aged.

*Our Ancestors gave the great Council of the State the Title of* ***Senate****, as consisting of a Body of* ***Senes****, or Old-Men, as the Word imports.*

Thus in a Play of the Poet [30]Nævius, where one asks this Question, "But how happen'd it, that in so small a Compass of Time you overset and lost so great a Government?" The Answer is, "A Parcel of young, raw and ignorant Orators started up, who took upon them to act the Statesmen; and found Means to insinuate themselves with, and manage the People." For 'tis a Truth but too well known, that Rashness attends Youth, as Prudence does Old Age.

# VII.

BUT IT is alledged, that Memory fails in Old Age. That it does so, I freely grant; but then it is principally, where it has not been properly exercised; or with those who naturally have no Strength of Brain: For such as have, will pretty well retain it. [31]Themistocles could call every Citizen of Athens by his Name; and do you think, when he became old, that if he met Aristides, he would salute him by the Name of Lysimachus?

For my own Part, I not only know these who are now living, but I remember their Fathers and Grandfathers: Nor when I read over the Inscriptions of the Tombs, do I find I am in Danger of losing mine. I never yet heard of an Old Man that forgot where he had hid his Treasure.

The Oldest will remember what engages their Thoughts and Care, as when they give or take Security, with such other Affairs as concern them. How do the Lawyers, the Pontiffs, the Augurs, and the Philosophers, who live to a great Age? What a vast Number of Particulars must all these comprehend in their Memories? Men will retain their Understanding and Abilities, while they continue their Application and Diligence.

This we find true, not only in Men of great and publick Characters, but in those also, who have lived a quiet and unactive Life, and spent it only in Study. [32]Sophocles wrote Tragedies at a very great Age: And when his Sons, apprehending that through his Application to that Business alone, he neglected all his other Affairs, and consequently they would be ruined; they cited him to the Court, that (as you know it is with us, when People by their ill Conduct ruin their Estate, it is taken from them, and committed to better Hands; so) the Judges of Athens should take the same Order with him, as become uncapable of Business: He is said to have read to the Judges a Part of his Tragedy, called *Oedipus Coloneus*, that he had then in Hand, and to have asked them, whether they thought that the Work of a Dotard: Upon which they acquitted him.

*I never yet heard of an Old Man that forgot where he had hid his Treasure.*

Consider then, whether Age can be truly said to destroy the Capacity or extinguish the Abilities of the Mind. Was this Man, was [33]Hesiod, was [34]Simonides, or [35]Stesichorus, or those I mention'd before, Isocrates and Gorgias or [36]Homer? Or were those Princes of the Philosophers, [37]Pythagoras, or [38]Democritus, or [39]Plato, or [40]Socrates, or those who came afterwards, [41]Zeno and [42]Cleanthes, or he, whom you yourselves have seen in Rome, [43]Diogenes the Stoic; I say, Were any of these disabled by Age, or did it oblige them to Silence? Did they not all, without sinking under it, continue their Studies as in Youth, to the last of their Days, and to an extream Old Age?

*How do the Lawyers, the Pontiffs, the Augurs, and the Philosophers, who live to a great Age? Men will retain their Understanding and Abilities, while they continue their Application and Diligence.*

But to insist no longer on those diviner Studies, that may perhaps communicate a Vigour to both Mind and Body, and to descend to low and common Life; I can name several old Countrymen of my particular Acquaintance in this Sabine Neighbourhood, who never on account of their Age, decline their Business; nor ever have any considerable Work carried on, either in Planting, Sowing, Reaping or Storing, but they are themselves at the Head of it: Tho' you may say, this is not so much to be wondered at, in the Business of the Year, because (as 'tis said) no Man thinks himself so old, but that he may live one Year longer: But this alone is not the Case with these Men I speak of; they take not Pains only in such Work, as they may expect themselves to reap the Fruits of; but they freely labour also in such as they are sure can produce none in their Time: They raise Nurseries, and plant Trees, for the Benefit only of another Generation, or, as our [44]Statius expresses it in his *Synephebi*, "They plant to profit a succeeding Age."

Nor, if you ask one of these Men, for whom it is he is thus labouring, will he be at any Loss to answer thus, I do it, he will say, for the Immortal Gods, who, as they bestow'd these Grounds on me, require at my Hands that I should transmit them improved to Posterity, who are to succeed me in the Possession of them.

## VIII.

THAT POET was much more just in what he said of an Old Man providing for his Successor, than in this other Saying of his:

> *Indeed were Age with no more Ills attended*
> *Than this alone, this were alone sufficient;*
> *That many Things by living long we see*
> *We never wish'd to see* ——

And I say, as probably, many Things we wish'd but scarce could hope, to see. But are we exempt from this in Youth, more than in Old Age? Do not Men in all Ages see Things happen that displease them? I take the same Poet to be yet more in the wrong, where he says,

> *But this in Age I think the worst of all,*
> *That old Folks find the World grows weary of them,*
> *And they become a Burthen to their Friends.*

On the contrary, I say, rather a Pleasure, if it is not their own Faults: For, as the wise and good are in Age delighted with the Company of young People of Sense and good Inclinations,

and nothing makes Age sit lighter on them, than the Regard and Esteem of such; so all young People, who desire to recommend themselves to the World by a virtuous Life and solid Accomplishments must of course be pleased with the Opportunity of improving themselves by the Advice and Informations of the most Experienced: And thus I judge it is, that I observe you to be no less pleased with my Conversation, than I truly am with yours.

But you see that Old Age is so far from becoming languid and unactive, that it is always stirring, ever employing itself about something or other; generally indeed about such Things as the Person has been most conversant in, in the former Part of his Life. Nay some are so very averse to Idleness, that they rather choose to be learning something new, as [45]Solon we see glorying of himself in his Elegies, that *daily learning something, he grew old*: As I also did, who, when I was well advanced in Years, applied myself to learn Greek, and studied both the Language and their Literature with such Eagerness, as if my Thirst for them were never to be satisfied; for I longed to be acquainted with their Affairs, and gain'd so much Knowledge in them, that from thence I have been able to cite the several Examples you have heard from me: Nay so strong a Bent I had that Way, that hearing Socrates in his Old Age had learned to play on the Fiddle (for Music with them was a reputable Exercise) I had almost got into the Humour of learning that too, but I declined it: However I took true Pains in their other Studies.

*Many Things we wish'd but scarce could hope, to see. But are we exempt from this in Youth, more than in Old Age?*

## IX.

I MUST further say, that I do not now so much as wish to have the Strength of Youth again (for this is another of the Charges against Old Age) more than I wish'd in Youth for the Strength of an Ox or Elephant. For it is our Business only to make the best Use we can of the Powers granted us by Nature, and whatever we take in Hand, to do it with all our Might.

How silly then, and unworthy of a Man, was that of [46]Milo of Croton; who, when weakned with Age, beholding the Athletæ (or Wrestlers) at their Exercises, he look'd on his own Arms, and with this Expression, *But these Arms are now dead that once*—— fell a crying: But the Trifler mistook; for not his Arms only, but rather himself was dead; since he never had any thing valuable in him, but the Strength of his Rack and Limbs; and if these were gone, the whole Man were gone with them. [47]Sextus Æmilius never made such Complaint, nor [48]Titus Coruncanius, who lived many Years before him, nor [49]Publius Crassus, more lately; whose Old Age was employed in framing and drawing up Laws for their Country, and who appeared rather to improve in Prudence and Knowledge to the last of their Days.

I own indeed that the Orator is not in all Respects so capable in Old Age as he was in Youth: For in that Business, not only Skill and Abilities of the Mind are required, but also Strength of Body and of the Lungs. Yet those who had a good Voice in their Youth, will not wholly lose it in Age: For tho' it abates in Strength, it acquires a kind of Softness and Fluency, that render it agreeable, You see my Years, and yet I have not lost mine. But even when it becomes low, and in some measure fails, the Gravity and Composure with which an Old Man sedately, yet eloquently, delivers himself, not only draws Attention, but gains the Favour of the Audience; or, if he can't depend on his own Utterance, he may however put it into the Mouth of a Scipio or a Lælius, and do good Service with it.

*I do not now so much as wish to have the Strength of Youth again than I wish'd in Youth for the Strength of an Ox or Elephant. For it is our Business only to make the best Use we can of the Powers granted us by Nature.*

For, what can be more honourable, what more desireable in Life, than to see Old Men waited on by Numbers of the Young, making their Court to them for their Advice and Instruction? For none, certainly, will deny, that the Aged are the best qualified for instructing of Youth, and training them up in the Knowledge, as well as animating them to the Discharge of every important Duty in Life; than which there can be nothing of greater Moment and Consequence, nor of greater Advantage to the Publick.

And indeed I have often thought [50]Cneius Scipio and Publius Scipio, and your two Grandfathers, [51]L. Æmilius and [52]P. Africanus extreamly happy on this Account, when I have seen them, walk thus attended by the Nobility of our City, who seem'd intirely to depend on them.

And I must ever think, that all those who spend their Time in improving others in Knowledge, and teaching the nobler Arts, when their natural Strength of Body fails them, are intituled to our highest Regard and Esteem; tho' it is undoubtedly true, that even this Decay is oftner owing to some unhappy Courses, and living too fast in Youth, than to the natural Effects of Old Age alone. For a libidinous and intemporate Life in Youth, will unavoidably deliver over the Body languid and enervate to succeeding Old Age. Cyrus in his Dying-Speech, as given us by Xenophon, denies that he ever found himself weaker in his Old Age, or less capable of performing any Duty, than he had been in his younger Years.

*And I must ever think, that all those who spend their Time in improving others in Knowledge, and teaching the nobler Arts, when their natural Strength of Body fails them, are intituled to our highest Regard and Esteem.*

And when I was a Boy, I remember [53]Lucius Metellus, who, having been created [54]*Pontifex Maximus* four Years after his second Consulate, continued his Presidence in that College twenty-two Years, appeared to the last as vigorous, as if he had not been sensible of any Decay. I need say nothing of myself; tho' you know it is a Privilege allowed old People to talk of themselves.

FOR DO not you observe in Homer, how Nestor is on all Occasions glorying of his own former Exploits? For he lived, 'tis said to three times the common Age of Man; that is, He lived to see three successive Generations: And yet he had no Reason to apprehend his being thought tiresome on these Subjects; since (as Homer says) his Discourse flow'd more sweet than Honey from his Tongue: And herein bodily Strength had no Share or Concern at all. Yet the Great [55]Commander of all the Greeks, never once wish'd, that he had ten Men in the Camp of Ajax's Strength and Courage, but ten such as Nestor: For by the Assistance of such Counsellors, he doubted not but Troy would soon fall.

But to return. I am now in my Eighty-fourth Year, and I wish indeed; I could boast the fame of myself as Cyrus did. Yet this I can truly say, that tho' I have not the same Strength of Body as formerly, when I [56]first served in the Punic War, or when I was Quæstor in it; or when Consul in Spain; or when Tribune to the Consul Glabrio, I fought at Thermopylæ: Yet, as you see, Age has not yet wholly unstrung me. The Senate finds

no Defect in such Abilities as are proper for that Place; these are not wanting at the Rostra; nor am I wanting to my Friends or my Clients.

For I never could approve of that old Proverb, tho' commended (I know) by some, which bids us be old betimes, if we would continue old long. On the contrary I would rather choose to be old for a less Time, or die sooner, than to make myself old before I truly am. I therefore keep myself constantly employed; and no Man, I believe, ever yet found me quite idle.

But I have not the Strength of one of you; nor have you the Strength of [57]Pontius the Centurion; is he therefore to be preferred to you? He who has but a moderate Share of Strength, and applies it properly to make the best Use of it, as far as it will go, I assure you will rarely have Occasion to complain for want of more. Milo is said to have entred the Olympic Field carrying an Ox on his Back: Now, if the Choice were given you, which would you prefer, Milo's Strength of Body, or Pythagoras's Abilities of Mind?

*I would rather choose to be old for a less Time, or die sooner, than to make myself old before I truly am. I therefore keep myself constantly employed.*

In short, while you have Strength, use it; when it leaves you, no more repine for the want of it, than you did when Lads, that your Childhood was past: or at the Years of Manhood, that you were no longer Boys. The Stages of Life are fixed; Nature is the same in all, and goes on in a plain and steady Course: Every Part of Life, like the Year, has its peculiar Season: As Children are by Nature weak, Youth is rash and bold; staid Manhood more solid and grave; and so Old-Age in its Maturity, has something natural to itself, that ought particularly to recommend it.

I suppose, Scipio, you hear how your Grandfather's Host [58]Massinissa, now at the Age of Ninety Years, employs his Time; that it is indifference to him, whether he walks or rides; if he sets out on a Journey on Foot, he will not mount; or if he gets on Horse-back, he will not light; that no Rain nor Weather can oblige him, when abroad, to cover his Head; and that, being thin of Body, he is so active, as in his own Person to discharge all the several Duties of his Station, as a King and a General.

*The Stages of Life are fixed; Nature is the same in all, and goes on in a plain and steady Course: Every Part of Life, like the Year, has its peculiar Season.*

You see therefore, that constant Exercise with Temperance will still preserve a competent Share of our pristine Vigour.

BUT ALLOWING it, that Old People lose their Strength, I say again, they do not want it. The Laws, their Administration, the Institutions and Discipline of our Ancestors, publick and private, are their proper Business; but from Employments that require Strength of Body in their Execution, we are exempted. It is therefore so far from being the Case with us, that more is expected from us than we are able to perform, that, to say the Truth, there is much less.

But it will be alledged, perhaps, that some People are so weakned with Age, that by it they are rendred uncapable of every kind of Business whatsoever: To which I answer, That this is not so much the Fault of Age, as of Constitution, or the want of Health, which happens to all Ages. How weakly was Publ. Africanus's Son, he who adopted you, Scipio: He was all his Life so exceedingly infirm, that he scarce ever knew what Health was: Tho' had he not been unfortunate in that particular, he might otherwise have proved another Glory to our State; for he had not only all his Father's Greatness of Soul, but the further Advantage also of having that adorn'd

*We must prepare ourselves, my Friends, against Old Age; and as it is advancing, endeavour by our Diligence to mitigate and correct the natural Infirmities that attend it: We must use proper Preservatives.*

with the politest Literature. What Wonder is it then, if some Old Men labour under Weakness, since the Youngest, we see, cannot escape it?

We must prepare ourselves, my Friends, against Old Age; and as it is advancing, endeavour by our Diligence to mitigate and correct the natural Infirmities that attend it: We must use proper Preservatives, as we do against Diseases; great Care must, in the first Place, be taken of our Health; all bodily Exercise must be moderate, and especially our Diet; which ought to be of such a kind, and in such Proportion, as may refresh and strengthen Nature, without oppressing it.

Nor must our Care be confined to our Bodies only; for the Mind requires much more, which without it will not only decay, but our Understanding will as certainly die away in Old Age, as a Lamp not duly supplied with Oil. The Body, we know, when overlaboured, becomes heavy, and, as it were, jaded; but 'tis Exercise alone that supports the Spirits, and keeps the Mind in Vigour. Hence it is, that you see Old Men disadvantageously represented by Cæcilius, and other Comic Poets on the Stage, when the Characters of weak and credulous, or dissolute Old Fellows, are exposed to Contempt and Ridicule: But these are the Vices only of such as, when grey with Years, abandon themselves to Idleness and Extravagance, and not of Old Age itself. For as Wantonness and loose Desires are more peculiar to Youth than to the Aged; and yet not to all Youth, but to such only as are by Nature viciously inclined, or

have been loosely educated; So that silly Dotishness, that is imputed to Old Age, will be found only in Persons of weak and abject Spirits.

Appius had four stout Sons, and five Daughters; yet tho' he was very old, and blind besides, he was able not only to govern that great Family, but also to manage his large Dependencies of Clients: He kept his Mind ever intent upon his Affairs, without flagging or bending under his Age, and maintained not only an Authority, but a Command over his People: His Servants stood in Awe of him; his Children revered him, and they all loved him; and that whole Family constantly kept up to the sober and strict Discipline derived to them by Succession from their Ancestors. Thus Old Age is ever honourable, where it takes Care to support its proper Rights, and gives them not weakly away, but asserts them to the last. For, as we commend such Youths, as shew something of the Solidity of Age; so we do the same by the Aged, who express the Liveliness of Youth: And whoever pursues this Method, tho' he may become old and decayed in Body, will never be so in Mind, nor be found so in his Understanding.

*Nor must our Care be confined to our Bodies only; for the Mind requires much more, which without it will not only decay, but our Understanding will as certainly die away, as a Lamp not duly supplied with Oil.*

I am now on the seventh Book of my *Origines,* [59]wherein I am collecting all the Monuments of Antiquity of every kind. I am also making out those Orations, that I formerly delivered in pleading the several Causes I defended. I am further treating of the Civil Law, and of that of the Augurs and Pontiffs. I read much Greek, and, agreeable to the Pythagorean Precept, the

*I read much Greek, and, agreeable to the Pythagorean Precept, the better to exercise my Memory, I recollect at Night what I have heard, said or done in the Day.*

better to exercise my Memory, I recollect at Night what I have heard, said or done in the Day. These are the Methods I pursue to keep my Mind employed; and while with a constant and assiduous Application I continue these Exercises, I cannot say I am sensible of any Want of Strength. I am still able to serve my Friends; I come duly to the Senate, and there propose such Matters of Weight, as I have long pondered and digested; and I support what I propose with Arguments, to which bodily Strength can contribute nothing.

And if for want of a competent Share of that Strength, I should be rendered uncapable of all this; yet I could please myself, even on my Couch, with running them over in my Thoughts. And whoever will pursue the same Methods, and practice thus, will scarce be sensible of the Advances of Old-Age, but gradually sliding on, and insensibly decaying, without any sudden Changes, will at last drop like ripe Fruit, or go off like an expiring Light.

# XII.

THE THIRD Charge against Old-Age was, That it is (they say) insensible to Pleasure, and the Enjoyments arising from the Gratifications of the Senses. And a most blessed and heavenly Effect it truly is, if it eases of what in Youth was the sorest and cruellest Plague of Life. Pray listen, my good Friends, to an old Discourse of [60]Archytas the Tarentine, a great and excellent Man in his Time, which I learned when I was but young myself, at Tarentum, under Fabius Maximus, at the Time he recovered that Place.

"The greatest Curse, the heaviest Plague, said he, derived on Man from Nature, is bodily Pleasure, when the Passions are indulged, and strong inordinate Desires are raised and set in Motion for obtaining it. For this have Men betray'd their Country; for this have States and Governments been plunged in Ruin; for this have treacherous Correspondences been held with publick Enemies: In short, there is no Mischief so horrid, no Villany so execrable, that this will not prompt to perpetrate. And as Adultery, and all the Crimes of that Tribe, are the natural Effects of it; so of course are all the fatal Consequences

*'Tis owned, that the most noble and excellent Gift of Heaven to Man, is his Reason: And 'tis as sure, that of all the Enemies Reason has to engage with, Pleasure is the most capital, and the most pernicious.*

that ensue on them. 'Tis owned, that the most noble and excellent Gift of Heaven to Man, is his Reason: And 'tis as sure, that of all the Enemies Reason has to engage with, Pleasure is the most capital, and the most pernicious: For where its great Incentive, Lust, prevails, Temperance can have no Place; nor under the Dominion of Pleasure, can Virtue possibly subsist."

That this might appear more plain, he desired his Hearers to form to themselves the Idea of a Person in the highest Raptures, enjoying the most exquisite Pleasures that could be conceived; and then try whether they could so much as imagine, such a Person in that State of Enjoyment, capable of Reflection, or making any more Use of his Reason, than if he were intirely divested of it. He therefore insisted, that nothing was more detestable, nothing more directly destructive to the Dignity of Man, than the Pursuit of bodily Pleasure, which it is impossible to indulge to a Height, and for a Continuance, without damping or extinguishing all the brighter Faculties of the Soul, and all the Powers and Light of the Understanding.

This Discourse our Host Nearchus of Tarentum, who had continued firm in the Roman Interest after that City was betrayed to Annibal, said, Archytas had used to Caius Pontius the Samnite, the Father of Pontius [61]who beat our Consuls Spurius Posthumius and Titus Veturius at Caudium; that their old Men had handed down the Relation to them, and that Plato of Athens was present at the time; which is probable enough; for I find Plato was at Tarentum the Year that [62]Lucius Æmilius and Appius Claudius were Consuls.

Now this Discourse I repeat to you, that from hence you may learn, how much those, who cannot as they ought in their Strength of Age resist the Allurements of Pleasure, are afterwards obliged to their Years, that cure them of their irregular Inclinations they had not before the Power to correct. For all Voluptuousness is undoubtedly an Enemy to Reason; it obstructs wise Counsels, blinds the Understanding, and is in its own Nature inconsistent with true Virtue.

It was with great Uneasiness to myself, that when Censor, I turned [63]Lucius Flaminius, Brother to that Great Man Titus Flaminius, out of the Senate, seven Years after he had himself been Consul. But I could not bear, that such a scandalous Instance of his Dissoluteness should pass without public Censure. For while he as Consul commanded the Army in Gaul, to please a lewd Strumpet he carried with him, he caused one of the Prisoners who were under Sentence of Death, to be brought in before them, and there, to gratify her in her barbarous Request, that she might see a Man put to Death, he struck off his Head on the Spot. His Brother Titus being then Censor, this was not in his Time taken Notice of; but when Flaccus and I succeeded him, we judged it incumbent on us, in Discharge of our Trust, to exert the Authority of our Office, and brand with Ignominy an Action so detestable, that it not only involved the Actor himself in Infamy, but also cast a Reproach on the whole State.

*For all Voluptuousness is undoubtedly an Enemy to Reason; it obstructs wise Counsels, blinds the Understanding, and is in its own Nature inconsistent with true Virtue.*

## XIII.

I HAVE often heard our Old Men, who said they had it from their Elders, relate, that Caius Fabricius, when he was sent Embassador to Pyrrhus, to redeem the Captives, was strangely surprized, when [64]Cineas the Orator, who attended Pyrrhus, told him, there was in Athens a great Professor of Wisdom, who laid it down as his Grand Principle, that all we do should be directed only to Pleasure; and that [65]M. Curius and [66]Titus Coruncanius hearing this from Fabricius, used to wish, that Pyrrhus and the Samnites could be converted to that [67]Professor's Religion; for then it would cost Rome much less Trouble to master them. M. Curius was for some Time Contemporary with [68]Publius Decius, who five Years before Curius was the first time Consul, had in his own fourth Consulate devoted himself for the publick Safety. Fabricius and Coruncanius living in the same Age with him, must also have known him well. And all these, not only by their own Conduct, shewed their firm Perswasion, but they were further confirmed in it by that Action of Decius, That there is something truly great and excellent in its own Nature worthy

to be contended for, and which all good Men would, in Despite of all the Allurements of Pleasure, for its own sake pursue, and labour to obtain.

Thus I judged it necessary to be the more full on this Head of Pleasure, and shew the Dangers of it, to the end you might clearly see, it is so far from being a Disadvantage to Old-Age, its Palling our Inclinations to Pleasure, that on the contrary it is rather a great and valuable Blessing. For if it is in a good Measure dead to the Enjoyments others find in Banqueting, sumptuous Feasts and Carousings, it is freed at the same time from all the troublesome Effects of these; as Fumes, Crudities, uneasy Sleep, or the want of it; with divers other such like Disorders.

*'Tis with too much Justice that the divine Plato calls it the Bait of Evil, by which Men are caught as Fish with a Hook.*

Yet as Nature has so ordered it, that Pleasure should have a very strong Hold of us, and the Inclination to it appears deeply founded in our very Composition, (and 'tis with too much Justice that the divine Plato calls it the Bait of Evil, by which Men are caught as Fish with a Hook;) therefore, though Age is not taken, nor can well bear, with those splendid sumptuous Feastings and Revels, yet we are not so insensible to the Pleasures of Life, but that we can indulge ourselves, and take a real Delight in sober and temperate Entertainments with our Friends.

I remember, when I was a Boy, I often saw [69]Caius Duillius, Marcus's Son, who gained the first Victory over the Carthaginians at Sea, returning home from Supper with Torches and Music

*Our Ancestors very wisely called those Meetings of Friends to eat and drink together, by the Name of* ***Convivium****: A Term much more proper than that of the Greeks, whose Name imports nothing but Eating and Drinking together.*

before him; a Practice that he thought fit (tho' without any Precedent for it) to continue in his private Station: So great was the Pleasure he gave himself, tho' not without some Vanity, in keeping up the Memory of that great Action.

But why should I quote others, and not rather return and speak of myself? In my Youth I had always a Set of select Companions; for those Societies or Clubs now in Practice, took their Beginning when I was Quæstor, at the Time the [70]Mother of the Gods was brought to Rome. My Friends and I then had our Meetings and Collations duly; but these were always moderate, tho' it was at an Age when our Blood was warm, which inevitably cools as Years come on. Nor did I ever measure my Pleasure in those Entertainments by any sensual Gratifications whatever, but solely by the Conversation or Discourses we held on various Subjects. For our Ancestors very wisely called those Meetings of Friends to eat and drink together, by the Name of *Convivium*, or Living-together; as if Society were the Design of them: A Term much more proper than that of the Greeks, whose Name for them imports nothing but Eating and Drinking together; as if they preferred that Part of the Entertainment, which is truly in itself the least valuable.

## XIV.

IN SUCH regular Entertainments, when seasonable, I own, I have always, in View of what I have mention'd, taken a sensible Pleasure: Nor do I choose for my Companions only Persons about my own Age; for of these there are now very few left; but those also of yours. And I think myself much obliged to my Age, that it has encreased my Inclination for Discourse and Conversation, and rendred the Business of Eating and Drinking a Matter still of more Indifferency to me.

Yet where others take a Pleasure even in these, that I may not be thought to declare War against all Gratifications of Sense, as Nature requires Refreshment, and Old-Age is not without its Relish; I think such Entertainments even for the sake of good Cheer, so far as this is comfortable to Nature, are very allowable, and may sometimes be indulged, when duly limited within the Bounds of Moderation.

But what now gives me the greatest Pleasure in these Cases, is to practice the Method instituted by our Ancestors, that is, That the Conversation should turn on Subjects proposed by the Master of the Feast, and that the Cups should be moderate

*What now gives me the greatest Pleasure, is to practice the Method instituted by our Ancestors, That the Conversation should turn on Subjects proposed by the Master of the Feast, and that the Cups should be moderate and cooling, in a cool and shady Place.*

and cooling, in a cool and shady Place in Summer, as in that of [71]Xenophon; or in the Sun, or, if colder, by a good Fire in Winter: The Method that I now practice amongst my Sabine Neighbours, whom I frequently meet on such Occasions, and spend a good Part of the Night with them.

But to return to the Charge, It is alledged that Old Age is not sensible to that Titillation of Pleasure, that is found in the other Parts of Life; which is certainly true: But at the same time it has this great Advantage to ballance it, that it does not so much as wish to have it. Sophocles said well, who, when he was asked at a great Age, whether he had yet any Acquaintance with Venus, answered, Heavens forbid! I thank the Gods I am got rid of that Tyranny. Such as are addicted to those Pleasures, will think it hard to be debarred of them; but others, who have gone through, and are past them, find themselves happier in being deprived of the Inclination. Nor can any one be said to want, what he does not so much as wish for. And this State, I say, of not desiring, is preferable in itself even to that of enjoying.

'Tis true, that Men in their Prime have a greater Gust to all Pleasures; but then most of these are, in the first Place, but mean in themselves; and in the next, if Old Men have not the same to such a Height, they either desire them not at all, or they have a competent Share of such as are fit for them. As those, perhaps, who fit in the Pit at the Theatre, have more of the Pleasure in seeing [72]Turpio Ambivius act, than such as sit

at a greater Distance in the Galleries; yet these last, tho' they have less, are not wholly without theirs: So Youth, as it has a nearer Communication, and livelier Relish for Pleasure, may be more powerfully affected with it; yet those, whose Age has distanced them from the gayer Scenes of it, have their Share of Delight, and enjoy as much of it at least, as they crave or wish for.

For how solid, how sincere, think you, must that Pleasure be to the Mind, when, after it has happily work'd thro' the ruffling Tides of those uneasy Passions, Lust, Ambition, Emulation, Contention, and every strong impetutous Desire, it finds itself arrived at its Harbour, and like a Veteran discharged from the Fatigues of War, got home, and retired within itself into a State of Tranquility? But if it has the further Advantage of Literature and Science, and can by that Means feed on, or divert itself with some useful or amusing Study, no Condition can be imagined more happy than such calm Enjoyments, in the Leisure and Quiet of Old Age.

*Sophocles said well, who, when he was asked at a great Age, whether he had yet any Acquaintance with Venus, answered, Heavens forbid!*

How warm did we see [73]Gallus, your Father's intimate Friend, Scipio, in Pursuit of his Astronomical Studies to the last? How often did the rising Sun surprise him, fix'd on a Calculation he began over Night? And how often the Evening, on what he had begun in the Morning? What a vast Pleasure did it give him, when he could foretell to us, when we should see the Sun or Moon in an Eclipse? And how many others have we known in their Old Age delighting themselves

in other Studies? which, tho' of less Depth than those of Gallus, yet must be allowed to be in themselves ingenious and commendable?

How pleased was [74]Nævius with his Poem of the Punic War? And how [75]Plautus with his *Truculentus* and *Pseudolus*? I remember even Old Livius, who had his first Dramatic Piece acted six Years before I was born, in the Consulship of Cento and Tuditanus, and continued his Compositions till I was grown up towards the State of Manhood.

What need I mention [76]Licinius Crassus's Studies in the Pontificial and Civil Law? Or those of Publius Scipio, now lately made Supream Pontiff? And all these I have seen, not only diverting themselves in Old Age, but eagerly pursuing the several Studies they affected.

*How sincere must that Pleasure be to the Mind, when it finds itself arrived at its Harbour, and like a Veteran discharged from the Fatigues of War, got home, and retired within itself into a State of Tranquility?*

With what unwearied Diligence did we behold [77]Marcus Cethegus, whom Ennius justly enough called the Soul of Perswasion, applying himself at a great Age to Oratory, and the Practice of Pleading? Upon all which let me ask you, what Gratifications of Sense, what voluptuous Enjoyments in Feasting, Wine, Women or Play, and the like, are to be compared with those noble Entertainments? Those pure and serene Pleasures of the Mind, the rational Fruits of Knowledge and Learning, that grafted on a good natural Disposition, cultivated by a liberal Education, and trained up in Prudence and Virtue, are so far from being pall'd in Old Age, that they rather continually improve, and grow on the Possessor.

Excellent therefore was that Expression of Solon, which I mention'd before, when he said, *That daily learning something, he grew old*: For the Pleasures arising in such a Course, namely those of the Mind, must be allowed incomparably to exceed all others.

*Those pure and serene Pleasures of the Mind, the rational Fruits of Knowledge and Learning, that continually improve, and grow on the Possessor.*

## XV.

BUT I am now come to speak to the Pleasures of a Country-Life, with which I am infinitely delighted. To these Old Age never is an Obstruction. It is the Life of Nature, and appears to me the exactest Plan of that which a wise Man ought to lead. Here our whole Business is with the Earth, the common Parent of us all, which is never found refractory, never denies what is required of it, nor fails to return back what is commited to it with Advantage, sometimes indeed with less, but generally with a very large Interest.

Nor is it the View of this Increase only which yields Delight, but there arises yet a greater from a Contemplation of the Powers of the Earth, and Vegetation: For to me it is most affecting to behold, how, when the Soil is duly laboured and mellowed, and receives after harrowing the scattered Seed into its genial Bosom, warmed with due Heats and Vapours, it there cherishes it in its vital Embraces; and then opening, shoots it upwards, and rears it into a verdant Blade; which taking fast Hold with its fibrous Roots below, springs up into a jointed Stalk, preparing new Seed again in its Cells, which gradually

enlarges from the Ear, with the Grain exactly ranged in decent Rows; and is secured with Awns, to defend it from the Rapine of the little Birds, that would otherwise assail and make Prize of it.

But why should I enter into Particulars, or observe upon the first Planting, Shooting and Growth of the delicious Vine? I should never have done, if I indulged myself in representing at large the Pleasure I take in these Solaces of my Old Age. Nor must I dwell on that plastic Power seen in all the Productions of the Earth, which from so small a Grain in the Fig, or the little Stone of a Grape, or from the minute Seeds of others, raises up such bulky Trunks with their shady Heads and extended Branches. But who can consider the Variety in the Methods of Propagation, by Shoots, Sprouts, Loppings, Quicksets and Slips, without being seized at the same time with Admiration and Delight?

*The little Bud pushes out the new Shoot, whereon the tender young Grape is formed; which gradually swelling by Nourishment from the Earth, is at first austere to the Taste...*

The Vine, that naturally runs low, and cannot rear itself without a Support, is for this end provided with Tendrils, by which, like so many Hands, it lays hold on every thing it meets with, that may raise it; and by these Aids expands, and becomes so luxuriant, that to prevent its running out into useless Wood, the Dresser is obliged to prune off its superfluous wandring Branches: After which, from the standing Joints, in the ensuing Spring, the little Bud, called the Gem, pushes out the new Shoot, whereon the tender young Grape is formed; which gradually swelling by Nourishment from the Earth, is at first austere to the Taste, but, guarded with Leaves around, that it may neither want due Warmth, nor suffer by too scorching Rays, it ripens by the Sun's enlivening Beams, and acquires that delicious Sweetness and beautiful Form, that equally please both the Taste and Eye; and then enriches the World with that noble Liquor, the Advantages of which I need not name.

Yet it is not the Sense of these, nor of all the Advantages of Husbandry, as I have said, that so nearly affects me, as the Pleasure I find in their Culture alone: Such as ranging the Vines, and their supporting Perches in exact and even Rows, in arching and binding their Tops, lopping off the woody and barren, and training and encouraging the fruitful Branches, to supply every Vacancy; and then contemplating the Beauty and Order with the Process of Nature in the Whole. What need I mention the Pleasure of improving the more barren Grounds, and rendring them fruitful, by bringing down Water in refreshing Rills, on the over-dry; and as carefully carrying it off from the wet and sunken; or by digging, and repeatedly trenching, to render them mellow? Or of the Advantages of Manure, of which I treated in my [78]Book of Husbandry, tho' the learned [79]Hesiod, amongst his Rules on that Subject, has not one Word of it. And yet Homer, whom I take to have lived some Ages before him, makes Old Laertes divert the Thoughts of his Son Ulysses's Abscence, by rustic Labours and [80]Dunging the Fields.

*...but acquires that delicious Sweetness and beautiful Form, that equally please both the Taste and Eye; and then enriches the World.*

But besides the Pleasures already mentioned, from Corn-Fields, Meads and Vines, there is yet a vast Fund for others,

from Orchards, Cattle, Bees, and Gardens, with the endless Varieties of beautiful Flowers, that yield an Entertainment ever new and ever delighting: For in Orchards there arises a Pleasure not only from the Ranges of fruitbearing Trees, all answering to the View in just and exact Order; but above all, from their Improvement by Grafting; the finest Invention, in my Opinion, in Husbandry.

*Homer makes Old Laertes divert the Thoughts of his Son Ulysses's Abscence, by rustic Labours and Dunging the Fields.*

# XVI.

I COULD with Pleasure further proceed in enumerating many other Recreations, and delightful Entertainments the Country yields; but I am sensible I have dwelt rather too long on these already. You will however excuse me, I hope, and impute it in Part to the Pleasure the Agreeableness of the Subject yields me; and in some Part also, if you please, to the Talkativeness of Old Age; a Fault that, I must acknowledge, even while I am defending it, most commonly attends it.

But thus employed [81]Manius Curius, after he had triumphed over the Samnites and Sabines and Pyrrhus, spent his Old Age here in my Neighbouring Farm; which as often as I view, I am seized with Wonder, but can never sufficiently admire, either the great Moderation of the Man, or the regular Discipline of his Time. Curius, as he sat one Evening by his Fire-Side, met with a tempting Encounter: The Samnites, for whom he was too hard in the Field, in Hopes of softning him, sent him a large Present of Gold; but he with a brave Disdain rejecting it, sent back the Messengers with this Answer only, That he wanted none of their Gold, but thought it much more

glorious to command those who valued it, than to possess it himself. Now, could so great a Soul fail, think you, of making his Years easy to himself, and agreeable at any Age?

But to return to a Country-Life, that I may not quit the Subject I am upon, I mean, my own Old-Age: In those Days the Senators, that is, the *Senes*, or Old-Men of the State, dwelt in the Country, and lived on their Farms, [82]L. Quinctius Cincinnatus was at his Plow, when he was called to take upon him the supream Office of Dictator. This also was he, by whose Command his Master of the Horse, Servilius Hala, put Spurius Mælius to Death, for attempting at sovereign Power, and to make himself Absolute in the City. So Curius, and many others of those brave Old Men, were called from time to time off their Farms, to take upon them the highest Trusts and Charges in the State or War: And from hence it is, that the Serjeants or Messengers that wait on the Senate, first had, and to this Day retain their Name of *Viatores*, or Way-Men. Now, can we imagine that those great Men found themselves distressed by Old Age, while they would thus in the Country give themselves up to all the Variety of delightful Employments, that the Business of it either furnishes or requires?

*But he with a brave Disdain rejecting it, sent back the Messengers with this Answer only, That he wanted none of their Gold, but thought it much more glorious to command those who valued it, than to possess it himself.*

As for me, I must own, I think it impossible that any other kind of Life whatever can exceed it. For besides that Mankind cannot possibly subsist without it, there is not only a vast Pleasure derived from viewing and considering the Particulars I have mentioned, but it also fills the Heart with Joy to behold, how by proper Care and Management every thing is produced in Abundance, that can be subservient either to the Support and real Necessities of human Life, or even to the Pleasures and Delectation of it, as well as what is required for the Service of the immortal Gods.

Those therefore who make Pleasure their Aim, and think there is no other Good in Life, may here effectually find it. For can there be a greater than to see our Labours crowned with full Granaries, our Cellars with Wine, Oil, Honey, and all kind of Provisions? Our Dairies with Cheese; and Plenty of Pigs, Kid, Lambs and Fowl around us?

Our Gardens also are, as the Country-People call it, a lasting Flitch, from whence they may constantly cut, and it as constantly supplies them. Here also at suitable Times are our Labours seasoned with the agreeable and innocent Diversions of Hunting and Fowling; to say nothing of the delightful Prospect of Meadows in their Verdure, and Groves of planted Trees; as well as those of Vines and Olives that have been mention'd already.

*It also fills the Heart with Joy to behold, how by proper Care and Management every thing is produced in Abundance, as well as what is required for the Service of the immortal Gods.*

But I shall wind up, with observing, That as there is nothing more profitable, so there is not in Nature, in my Opinion, any thing more beautiful or affecting, than to behold a Plantation, with all the Parts of it, in compleat and perfect Order. And this, as I have said, is a Pleasure, that Old-Age is so far from being uncapable of enjoying, that it is by a kind of Impulse of Nature solicited and drawn to it. For no where else

can it meet with such suitable Entertainments. Here the cool Shades and refreshing Breezes, with purling Streams, invite abroad to pass the Summer's sultry Heats; and here good rousing Fires furnish large Provision against the colder Blasts of Winter.

*To others therefore we can freely resign all other Diversions, only, if they please, they may leave us Checquers and Tables.*

To others therefore we can freely resign all other Diversions, in Arms and Horses, with their military Exercises and all their Accoutrements, their Tennis, and every other Sport; only, if they please, they may leave us Checquers and Tables; or even these also we can give up; since Old Age can be very easy and very happy without any such trifling Amusements.

# XVII.

ALL THE Writings of Xenophon are on many Accounts highly useful; and I would advise you diligently to read them; which I doubt not but you do of yourselves. How fully and excellently does he, in that Book called his *Oeconomics*, set out the Advantages of Husbandry and a Country-Life? And that you may see he thought no Employment so fit for a King as this, Socrates there discoursing with Critobulus, tells him, that when Lysander of Lacedemon, a Person of great Merit, went to Cyrus the Younger, King of the Persians, at Sardis, with the Presents their Allies had collected; Cyrus entertaining him with great Courtesy and Civility, shewed him a Garden planted with extream Elegance; in which Lysander observing the beautiful Forms of the Trees in their Ranges, exactly disposed in the quincuncial Order; the Cleanness and Neatness of the Walks and Borders, and the delicious Fragrancy of the Flowers that breath'd all around their refreshing Odours; he was greatly taken with them all: But above all the rest, he said, he admired the Ingenuity of the Man, who had designed, and with so much Art and Skill disposed the Whole.

This is all my own Doing, said Cyrus; the Design was mine, I mark'd and measured out the Walks and Rows, and many of the Trees I planted with my own Hands. Then Lysander observing also at the same time the Neatness of his Person, and viewing his Purple, with the Richness of his Attire, set off, after the Persian Manner, with much Gold and Jewels, said, They may justly call you happy, Cyrus, since you are at the same time both good and great; your Virtue and your Fortune equally adorn each other.

And this Happiness, I say again, is left for Old Men to enjoy; nor can Age or any Length of Years disable them, while they have Health and Strength to walk, from enjoying, to their last Period, those sweet Amusements and Diversions, that rural Scenes and the Employments of a Country-Life afford.

*Nor can Age or any Length of Years disable them from enjoying those sweet Amusements and Diversions, that rural Scenes and the Employments of a Country-Life afford.*

We find that [83]Marcus Corvinus lived to a Hundred Years, and spent his last Days in Agriculture on his Farm. Between his first and last Consulate there were fourty-six Years; he therefore was engaged in public Employments and Trusts of Honour the full Term [84]that our Ancestors set for the Commencement of Old-Age. But, in this, his latter Days were more happy and glorious than his preceding Life, that he was more illustrious in himself, and clothed with a greater Authority freed from the Toil that commonly attends it: For Authority I esteem the Crown and Glory of Old-Age.

How conspicuous did this appear in [85]L. Cæcilius Metellus? And how in [86]Atilius Calatinus? on whom many Nations agreed

*His latter Days were more happy and glorious than his preceding Life, that he was more illustrious in himself, and clothed with a greater Authority freed from the Toil that commonly attends it.*

in conferring this great and noble Character, That *He was the worthiest Man of his Country*; as it is fully declared in that Copy of Verses now inscribed on his Tomb, which therefore are well known. Justly then might he be accounted honourable and great, in whose Praises the Voices of all Nations conspired.

How deservedly great did the late Supream Pontiff, Publius Crassus, as also his Successor in the same Dignity, [87]Marcus Lepidus, appear to us all? Why should I again mention Paulus, or Africanus, or Maximus? Who all bore so great an Authority with the People, that not only their Opinions when declared, but even their Looks and Nods carried an Awe with them, and in a manner commanded Submission.

Old-Age in a Person graced with Honours, is attended with such Respect and Authority, that the Sense of this alone is preferable to all the Pleasures Youth can enjoy.

# XVIII.

YET IN all I have said, I desire to be understood to mean the Old-Age of such Persons only, as have in their Youth laid solid Foundations for Esteem in advancing Years; for on no other Terms ought we to expect it. And hence it was, that what I once said in a publick Speech, met with so general an Applause, when I observed, That miserable was that Man's Old-Age, who needed the Help of Oratory to defend him.

Grey Hairs and Wrinkles avail nothing to confer the Authority I am here speaking of: It must be the Result of a Series of good Actions, and nothing but a Life honourably and virtuously led, thro' all the advancing Steps of it, can crown Old-Age with this blessed Harvest of its past Labours. Nor are those common Marks of Respect, tho' but of little Moment in themselves, to be altogether slighted; such as Morning-Salutations; to have the Way or Upper-hand given; to be waited on home or from home, and to be consulted; which, both with us and in all well-regulated States, in Proportion as they are more or less so, are most strictly observed and practiced.

Lysander of Sparta, whom I lately mentioned, was wont to say, That Lacedemon was of all Places the most honourable Sanctuary for Old-Age: For nowhere in the World is a greater Deference paid to Years, and in no Place Grey Hairs more reverenced and regarded.

I find this also related, That a very old Man coming into the Theatre at Athens, to see the Play, and the Throng being so great, that he could find no Room nor Seat among his own Citizens, passing along towards that Part where the Embassadors of Lacedemon, then present, were placed; they all immediately rose up to give him a Seat: The Athenians observing this, clapt, and much applauded the Action; upon which one of the Spartans passed this just Reflection, That the Athenians (he perceived) knew very well what was right, but they knew not how to do it.

*What Satisfaction can all the Pleasures of Sensation taken together, yield, that will bear a Comparison with those the Mind must feel?*

There are many good Institutions in our College of Augurs, and particularly in this I am now speaking of, that the oldest Man always leads, and all the Members deliver their Opinions according to their Rank in Years; the Ancientest always taking Place, not only of such as have been in higher Posts than themselves, but even of those, who at the time bear the supream Command, and are at the Head of Affairs in the State. Now, what Satisfaction, think you, can all the Pleasures of Sensation taken together, yield, that will bear a Comparison with those the Mind must feel, from the Returns of reverencial Respect paid to the Authority of such an honourable Old Age?

Which whoever enjoys and rightly applies, seems to me to have well and happily performed in acting his Part in the Drama of Life, and at last like an approved Actor, he makes his last Part the best, and quits the Stage with an universal Plaudit.

*Some Wines sour with Age, while others grow better and richer. A Gravity with some Severity is to be allowed; but by no means Ill-nature.*

But it is said, People as they grow in Years, become more peevish, morose and passionate; and you may add covetous too: But, as I have said, these are the Faults of the Men, and not of Old Age. Yet something of a little Moroseness might probably, tho' not altogether justly, be excused; for they may sometimes be apt to think themselves slighted and play'd on; and further, a frail Body can bear but little, and therefore will be the sooner offended.

But all this may by proper Application be prevented or remedied: For by Reflection and a watchful Guard kept on the Motions of the Heart, natural Temper may be sweetned, and our Conduct softned. Of this we see frequent Instances in Life, and on the Stage a remarkable one in the two Brothers [88]in Terence's *Adelphi.* How rough and peevish is the one, how mild and good the other? And so the Case will generally hold.

Some Wines sour with Age, while others grow better and richer. A Gravity with some Severity is to be allowed; but by no means Ill-nature. What Covetousness in Old Men can mean, I must own, I cannot comprehend; for can any thing be more senselessly absurd, than that the nearer we are to our Journey's End, we should still lay in the more Provision for it?

# XIX.

WE ARE now come to the fourth and last Charge, which is thought most nearly to affect Old Age, and to give the greatest Anxiety of all others, *viz.* The Aproach of Death, which 'tis certain can be at no great Distance. But miserable is the Case of that Old Man, who in so long a Course of Years, has not laid in a sufficient Provision against those Fears, and enabled himself to contemn Death; which is either to be slighted, as being in Reality nothing in itself, in case it puts an intire End to us, Soul as well as Body; or else, it is to be valued, and to be desired and wish'd for, if it leads us into another State, in which we are to enjoy Eternity: And between these there can be no Medium.

What then am I to fear in Death, if after it, I am to have no Sense, and therefore can feel no Pain; or otherwise am to become immortal in another State by the Change? But again, can there be any one so void of Sense, as to think himself sure of living even to the next Evening? Nay, Youth in its greatest Vigour is subject to many more Casualties, and exposed to much greater and more frequent Dangers that may shorten

Life, than Old Age itself, which is allowed to be drawn so near its End. Their Heat of Blood, and the frequent Changes of Heats and Colds, which they undergo, render them more liable to Fevers and other Fits of Sickness, which, when they happen, bear heaviest on the strongest Constitutions; nor have they generally, when sick, the Patience to be so carefully nursed, as more elderly and experienced People. And from these and such like Causes it is, that we see so few attain to Old Age.

But happy would it be for the World, if more lived to reach it: For as Prudence and Skill are gained by Experience, and this depends on, and is enlarged by Length of Days; we might from greater Numbers of People grown old in such Experience, expect to see the Affairs of Life, both publick and private, more regularly administred: And indeed without some such, Government could scarce subsist at all.

*Can there be any one so void of Sense, as to think himself sure of living even to the next Evening?*

But to return to the Consideration of Death impending. How can that be accounted an Unhappiness peculiar to Old Age, which we well know is common, and frequently happens to the Youngest, as well as to the Old? I found by near Experience in my own [89]dear Son, and we saw in the Death of your [90]two Brothers, Scipio, who we expected were growing up to the highest Honours in Rome, that no Age is privileged, but Death is common to all. It may however be said, perhaps, that Youth has Room at least to hope they have Length of Life before them, which in Old Men would be vain. But foolish is that Hope: For what can be more absurd, than to build on utter Uncertainties, and account on that for sure, which probably may never happen?

And to what is alledged, that the Old Man has no Room left for Hope, I say, Just so much the happier is his Condition, than that of the Young; because he has already attained, and is sure of what the other only wishes and hopes for: The one wishes to live long, the other is at the End of that Wish, he has got it; for he has lived long already. Yet O good Gods! what is it in Life that can be said to be of long Duration? Tho' we should hold it to the utmost Extent of Age, or admit we should live the Days of that [91]Tartessian King, (for I have read that one Arganthonius reigned at Cadiz four-score Years, and lived to a hundred and twenty;) yet in my Opinion nothing can properly be termed lasting, that has a certain Period fixed: For when that is once come, all the past is over and gone; and in the Business of Life, when that is run out, nothing remains to us, but what results from past good and virtuous Actions. The Hours, and Days, and Months, and Years, all slide away, nor can the past Time ever more return, or what is to follow be fore-known.

*Prudence and Skill are gained by Experience, and this depends on, and is enlarged by Length of Days; indeed without some such, Government could scarce subsist at all.*

We ought all to be content with the Time and Portion assigned us. No Man expects of any one Actor on the Theatre, that he should perform all the Parts of the Piece himself: One Role only is committed to him, and whatever that be, if he acts it well, he is applauded. In the same Manner, it is not the Part

of a wise Man, to desire to be busy in these Scenes to the last Plaudit. A short Term may be long enough to live it well and honourably; and if you hold it longer, when past the first Stages, you ought no more to grieve that they are over, than the Husbandman repines that the Spring is past, and the Summer-Heats come on; or after these, the more sickly Autumn.

*What is it in Life that can be said to be of long Duration? Nothing can properly be termed lasting, that has a certain Period fixed: and nothing remains to us, but what results from past good and virtuous Actions.*

The Spring represents Youth, and shews what Fruits may be expected; the following Seasons are for ripening and gathering in those Fruits: And the best Fruits of Old Age are, as I have repeatedly said, the recollecting, and, as it were, feeding on the Remembrance of that Train and Store of good and virtuous Deeds, of which, in the Course of Life, we laid in a kind of Provision for this Season. But further we are to consider, that as all we enjoy is from Nature, whatever proceeds from, or is conformable to the established Laws of This, must in itself be good. Now, can any thing be more agreeable to those Laws, than that People in Old Age should die, since, more inconsistently with the Order of Nature, we find the same thing happens to Youth, even in the Prime of their Years?

But the Difference is great; for Young Men seem to be forced from Life, as Fires are extinguished by great Quantities of Water thrown on them; when on the contrary, Old Men expire of themselves, like a Flame when all its Fuel is spent. And as unripe Fruit requires some Force to part it from its native Bough; but when come to full Maturity, it drops of

*The best Fruits of Old Age are the recollecting and feeding on the Remembrance of that Train and Store of good and virtuous Deeds, of which, in the Course of Life, we laid in a kind of Provision.*

itself, without any Hand to touch it: So Young People die by something violent or unnatural; but the Old by meer Ripeness. The Thoughts of which to me are now become so agreeable, that the nearer I draw to my End, it seems like discovering the Land at Sea, that, after the Tossings of a tedious and stormy Voyage, will yield me a safe and quiet Harbour.

# XX.

ALL OTHER Stages of Life have their first Periods, at which they change into the next succeeding; but Old Age has no certain Limits; it may end sooner or later. All we have to do, is to live it well while it lasts, and do our best to discharge the respective Duties of our Station, with a just Contempt of Death, that, come when it will, we may without Surprize be prepared for it. And this will give Old Age more Courage and Resolution, than even Youth itself in its highest Vigour can pretend to. On this was [92]Solon's Answer to Pisistratus grounded, who, when asked by that [93]Tyrant, on what Foundation he built his Presumption in so boldly opposing him, answered, On his Age. [As if he should say, You can but take my Life, and of that there is now so little left, that it is not to be regarded.]

But the most desirable End of Life is, when with our Understandings clear, and our Senses intire, the same sovereign Power of Nature that formed us, again dissolves us. For, in our Frame, as in all other Things, Ships, Edifices, and the like, the Work is best taken to Pieces by the same Hand that first put it together: And as all Things with Age become crazy and tender, it is then done by much the easiest.

Thus Old People, for the little Remainder of Life that is left them, should stand loose and indifferent, neither anxious to have it prolonged, nor precipitantly or without just Cause to shorten it; remembring the Precept of Pythagoras, That no Man should quit his Post, but at the Command of his General, that is, of God himself. And in regard to those we are to leave behind us, tho' some have commended Solon for saying —— He wish'd not to die unmourned and unlamented by his Friends; in which his Sense doubtless was, that he desired while he lived to be loved and valued by them; Yet I know not but that of Ennius is altogether as just,

*Let none with Tears or Sighs my Funeral grace:*

For his Meaning was, that a Death crown'd with Immortality, ought by no means to be lamented.

*In our Frame, as in all other Things, Ships, Edifices, and the like, the Work is best taken to Pieces by the same Hand that first put it together.*

Again, if we consider the Article of Death, or the Pain supposed to attend it, we shall find, that in Dying there is either no Pain at all, or, if any, it is, especially to Old People, of a very short Continuance. And after it, there is either no Sense at all, (as I have said) or such as we have great Reason to wish for. But this is a Subject which concerns not Old Men alone: It is the Business of the Young as well as the Old, to meditate on Death, and to make the Thoughts of it so familiar to them, that in every Age they can despise it, and so guard themselves

against it, that it can never surprize them. Without this Provision 'tis impossible at any Stage of Life, to have the Mind free and easy; since no Man can be ignorant that he must die, nor be sure that he may not that very Day. How then can such as dread Death have, under such absolute Uncertainties, so much as one quiet Minute?

*Remembring the Precept of Pythagoras, That no Man should quit his Post, but at the Command of his General, that is, of God himself.*

But I need not dwell on this Head, when I reflect on our own History, and consider, not only such Examples of Intrepidity and a noble Contempt of Death; as that of [94]Lucius Brutus, who so bravely fell in defending the Liberties of his Country; or of the [95]two Decij, who devoting themselves for the Safety of it, pushed with their Horses into the midst of the Enemy, with no other View, than to be cut in Pieces; nor of [96]Marcus Atilius, who, to keep his Word to his Enemies, returned to certain Tortures and Death; or of the two [97]Scipio's, who, to obstruct the Passage of the Carthaginians, exposed and lost their own Lives; or of your Grandfather [98]Lucius Paulus (Scipio) who resolved by his own Death to atone for the Rashness of his Collegue, in our shameful Overthrow at Cannæ; or of [99]Marcus Marcellus, whose Death even the most inveterate of our Enemies thought fit to honour with a Funeral.

I say, I need not dwell on this Head of the Contempt of Death, when I reflect not only on the noble Instances of it in such Great Men as these, but even on those of our [100]Legions themselves (as I have noted in my *Origines*) who, when the Service or Honour of their Country called, have offered their

*Children have their particular Diversions; and does Youth, when past Childhood, pursue or desire the same?*

own Lives as Victims, and chearfully marched up to Posts, from which they knew there was no Probability they should ever return. Now, if Young Men, or those in the Vigour of Life, and many of them not only uncultivated by Learning, but meer Rusticks, who never had the Opportunity of Instruction, could so easily contemn Death; shall Old Men who have had the Advantage of Literature and Philosophy, be afraid of it?

By living long we come to a Satiety in all things besides, and this should naturally lead us to a Satiety of Life itself. Children we see have their particular Diversions; and does Youth, when past Childhood, pursue or desire the same? Youth also has its peculiar Exercises; and does full Manhood require these as before? Or has Old Age the same Inclinations that prevailed in more vigorous Years? We ought then to conclude, That as there is a Succession of Pursuits and Pleasures in the several Stages of Life, the one dying away, as the other advances and takes Place; so in the same Manner are those of Old Age to pass off in their Turn. And when this Satiety of Life has fully ripen'd us, we are then quietly to lie down in Death, as our last Resting-Place, where all Anxiety ends, and Cares and Fears subsist no more.

# XXI.

BUT WHY should I not speak freely, and without Reserve communicate my whole Thoughts on this Subject; of which as I am now drawing nearer to it, I seem to have a clearer Sense and View? I must say, then I am clearly of Opinion (Scipio and Lælius) that those great Men, and my very good Friends, your Fathers, tho' dead to us, do now truly enjoy Life, and such a Life as alone can justly deserve the Name. For while we are closed in these mortal Frames, our Bodies, we are bound down to a Law of Necessity, that obliges us with Labour and Pains to attend to the Discharge of the several incumbent Duties it requires. But our Minds are of a heavenly Original, descended from the blissful Seats above, thrust down and immersed into these gross Habitations of the Earth, a Situation altogether unsuitable to a divine and eternal Nature. But the immortal Gods, I believe, thought fit to throw our immortal Minds into these human Bodies, that the Earth might be peopled with Inhabitants proper to contemplate and admire the Beauty and Order of the Heavens, and the whole Creation; that from this great Exemplar they might form their Conduct and regulate their Lives, with the like unerring Steadiness, as we see is unvariably pursued, not only in those celestial Motions, but thro' the whole Process of Nature.

Nor have I been led into this Belief from my own Reasonings only, but by the Authority of those great and exalted Souls, the Philosophers who have lived before us. For I have heard, that Pythagoras and the Pythagoreans, whom I may call our [101]Countrymen; for their Habitation was in Italy, and thence they had the Name of the Italic Sect: I have heard, I say, that those Philosophers laid it down as their fixed and grand Principle, that our Minds are an Efflux or Portion of the Divine Universal Mind, that governs the Whole. I have also seen and considered the [102]Discourse that Socrates held with his Friends, the last Day of his Life, concerning the Immortality of the Soul: That Great Socrates, who was judged by Apollo's Oracle to be the wisest of Men.

*While we are closed in these mortal Frames, our Bodies, we are bound down to a Law of Necessity. But our Minds are of a heavenly Original, descended from the blissful Seats above.*

But my Conclusion is thus, and I am fully perswaded in myself, That a Being so active, and so swift in Thought, as to be confined by no Distance of Time or Place; that treasures up in Memory such Multitudes and Varieties of Things past, and from these also can form a Judgment of what is to ensue; that can comprehend within itself so many different Sciences and Arts; strike out new Inventions, and by fresh Discoveries still add to what has been known: Such a Being, I say, as is capable of all this, I am fully perswaded, can never be of a mortal Nature. For, as it is ever in Motion, yet is not put into it by any

thing extrinsic to itself, but it is It-Self the Spring of all its Motion; therefore, since it cannot depart or go out from itself, it must necessarily ever continue, and cannot end. Again, as it is in Nature simple and unmixt, without any Composition of different or dissimilar Parts, it cannot therefore be divided; and if not divided, it cannot be dissolved and die.

This seems also to be an Argument for the Pre-existence of Souls, and that they were endued with Knowledge, before they entred on this Stage; that Children so readily apprehend Things altogether new to them in this Life, learn many difficult Arts, and take in the Notions of Things, as if they were natural to them, and they were not now learning any thing new, but were only recollecting what they had known before. Thus Plato argues.

*I have also seen the Discourse that Socrates held with his Friends, the last Day of his Life, concerning the Immortality of the Soul: That Great Socrates, who was judged by Apollo's Oracle to be the wisest of Men.*

## XXII.

AND IN Xenophon, Cyrus the Elder in his last Discourse to his Children, expresses himself thus: Do not, my dear Children, imagine, that when I leave you, I shall be no more: For in the Time I have been with you, you could never see my Mind, but only knew by my Actions, that it was lodged in this Body. Be you therefore perswaded, that tho' you no longer see its Lodging, yet it still as surely exists, as before. For even the Fame and Honours of illustrious Men, could not, as we see they do, continue after Death, unless their Souls, by their Existence, in some Measure contributed to their Duration.

I never indeed could persuade myself, that Souls confined in these mortal Bodies, can be properly said to live, and that when they leave them, they die; or that they lose all Sense when parted from these Vehicles: But, on the contrary, when the Mind is wholly freed from all corporeal Mixture, and begins to be purified, and recover itself again; then, and then only, it becomes truly knowing and wise.

Further, when the Body is dissolved by Death, it is evident what becomes of all the several Parts of it; for every thing we

see returns to the Elements of which it was formed: But the Mind alone is never to be seen neither while it is actuating the Body, nor after it leaves it.

*When the Mind is wholly freed from all corporeal Mixture, and begins to be purified, and recover itself again; then, and then only, it becomes truly knowing and wise.*

You may further observe, that nothing so much resembles Death, as Sleep: But the Soul in Sleep, above all other Times, gives Proofs of its divine Nature: For when free, and disengaged from the immediate Service of the Body, it has frequently a Foresight of Things to come: From whence we may more clearly conceive what will be its State, when intirely freed from this bodily Prison.

Now, if the Case be thus, you are then to consider and honour me, as a Knowing Spirit: But if my Mind should also die with my Body, let it be your Care, first to pay all Reverence to the Gods, who support and govern this mighty Frame; and also, with a due and pious Respect for my Name, keep me always in your Remembrance.

Thus Cyrus on his Death-Bed.

XXIII.

AND NOW, to mention some of our own People. No Man, Scipio, shall ever prevail on me to believe, that either your Father Paulus, or two Grandfathers Paulus and Africanus, or Africanus's Father and his Uncle, or divers other illustrious Men, whom I need not name, would have undergone such vast Fatigues, to atchieve those glorious Actions which are consecrated to the Remembrance of all Posterity, if they had not clearly discerned, that they themselves had an Interest, and a kind of Right and Property in Posterity, by their still continuing to exist, and to be Sharers as well as Witnesses of their Fortune.

Do you imagine, that even I (for as I am an Old Man, I must talk a little of myself;) I say, that I would have undertaken such hazardous Attempts, and undergone such Fatigues by Day, such Toils by Night, at home and abroad, if I had supposed the Glory of my Actions must terminate with my Life, and all my Sense of it end with my being here? For if I had no further Views, might it not have been more eligible to me, to have past away my Days in Quiet and Ease, free from

Toils and Care, and without Labour or Contention? But my Spirit rousing in itself, I know not how, had Futurity always so much in View, as if it were assured, that as soon as it quitted this Life, it would then truly live, and not before.

And were it not really so that our Souls are immortal, why is it that the greatest of Men so ardently aspire to immortal Glory? Or why are the Wisest ever the most easy and content to die, and the Weak and Foolish the utmost unwilling? Is it not, think you, because the most Knowing perceive, they are going to change for a happier State, of which the more Stupid and Ignorant are uncapable of being sensible?

For my Part, I have a passionate Desire to see your Fathers again, whom I loved and honoured while here; and I not only long to meet those I knew and loved, but those illustrious Souls also, of whom I have heard and read, and have with Pleasure mention'd them in my Writings. Nor would I now on any Terms agree to be stopt in my Passage to them; no, not on Condition to be restored to the Bloom and Vigour of Youth again: Or should any heavenly Power grant me the Privilege of turning back, if I pleased, from this Age to Infancy, and to set out again from my Cradle, I would absolutely resist it; for as I have now got well nigh to the End of my Race, I should be extreamly unwilling to be called back, and obliged to start again.

*My Spirit had Futurity always so much in View, as if it were assured, that as soon as it quitted this Life, it would then truly live.*

For, if we consider Things aright, what is there in Life to make us fond of it? or that we can on solid Judgment

pronounce truly valuable? Or who is there, or ever has been, who has not at some Time or other met with Trouble and Anxiety sufficient to make him weary of it? This Comfort however attends the Thought, that the more the Satiety grows upon us, the nearer we approach to its End. I am therefore far from being of the Mind of some, and amongst them we have known Men of good Learning, who lament and bewail the Condition of human Life, as if it were a State of real Misery: For I am not at all uneasy that I came into, and have so far passed my Course in this World; because I have so lived in it, that I have Reason to believe, I have been of some Use to it; and when the Close comes, I shall quit Life as I would an Inn, and not as a real Home.

*Should any heavenly Power grant me the Privilege of turning back from this Age to Infancy, and to set out again from my Cradle, I would absolutely resist it; for as I have now got well nigh to the End of my Race, I should be extreamly unwilling to start again.*

For Nature appears to me to have ordain'd this Station here for us, as a Place of Sojournment, a transitory Abode only, and not as a fixt Settlement or permanent Habitation. But Oh the glorious Day, when freed from this troublesome Rout, this Heap of Confusion and Corruption below, I shall repair to that divine Assembly, that heavenly Congregation of Souls!

And not only to those I mentioned, but also to my dear Cato, than whom a more virtuous Soul was never born, nor did ever any exceed him in Piety and Affection. His Body I committed to the Funeral Pile, which he, alas! ought to have lived to do by mine: Yet his Soul did not forsake me, but keeping me still in View, removed to those Abodes, to which he knew, I was in a little Time to follow. I bore the Affliction

indeed with the Fortitude that became me, to outward View, tho' inwardly I severely felt the Pangs of it; but in this I have supported myself, that I knew our Parting was to be neither far nor long, and that the Time is but short till we shall happily meet again.

Now, these, my Friends, are the Means (since it was these you wanted to know) by which I make my Old-Age sit easy and light on me; and thus I not only disarm it of every Uneasiness, but render it even sweet and delightful. But if I should be mistaken in this Belief, that our Souls are immortal, I am however pleased and happy in my Mistake; nor while I live, shall it ever be in the Power of Man, to beat me out of an Opinion, that yields me so solid a Comfort, and so durable a Satisfaction. And if, when dead, I should (as some minute Philosophers imagine) be deprived of all further Sense, I am safe at least in this, that those Blades themselves will have no Opportunity beyond the Grave to laugh at me for my Opinion.

*Because I have so lived in it, that I have Reason to believe, I have been of some Use to it; and when the Close comes, I shall quit Life as I would an Inn, and not as a real Home.*

But whether immortal or not, or whatever is to be our future State; as Nature has set Limits to all its other Productions, 'tis certainly fit our frail Bodies also should at their proper Season be gathered, or drop into their Grave. And as the whole Course of Life but too much resembles a Farce, of which Old-Age is the last Act; when we have enough of it, 'tis most prudent to retire, and not to make a Fatigue of what we should endeavour to make only an Entertainment.

This is what I had to say of Old-Age; which I wish you also may live to attain, that you may from your own Experience, witness the Truth of the several Things I have now delivered you in this Conversation.

# *Notes*

# Notes for Chapter I

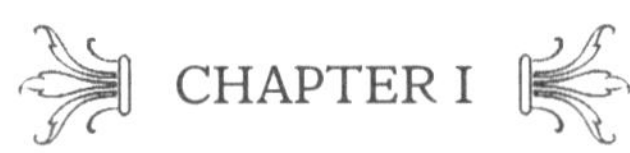

## CHAPTER I

Notes for page 2

1 Titus Pomponius Atticus, to whom this Discourse is address'd, was of an ancient Family of Rome, of the Equestrian Order, the second in Dignity amongst the Romans. Of all Cicero's Friends He appears to have been the most intimate and the most esteemed: For of the 36 Books now extant of Tully's Epistles, there are no less than 16, composing a distinct Tome, directed to Atticus alone. His Character in Life, as left us by his intimate Friend Cornelius Nepos, may be justly accounted the most beautiful we have received from Antiquity of either Greek or Roman. Nor does it appear to have been parallel'd in any Age. For tho' he liv'd in the Times of the greatest Factions and Divisions in Rome, as those of Sylla, Marius and Cinna, Cæsar and Pompey, Brutus and Cassius, with Anthony, Lepidus and Octavius (afterwards Augustus,) he conducted himself with such consummate Prudence and Integrity, that tho' caress'd by all, he neither joined with, nor offended any of them. But being possess'd of a vast Estate, neither acquired on his Part, nor improved by any lucrative Measures whatsoever; for his Patrimony was about the Value of 160 thousand Pounds Sterling; and by the Will of a surly Uncle, whom none besides could please, he receiv'd about 800 thousand more, with many other Legacies from his Friends and Admirers: Of this vast Estate, I say, besides his annual Expence on a genteel and hospitable, yet frugal Table, he spent the greatest Part in relieving the Distressed of every Party (as each had their Turns, Octavius excepted) without any other Distinction than that of their Worth and Wants; and without any Conditions or Expectation of Retribution.

# Notes for Chapter I

Notes for page 2

In his Youth, to avoid being engaged by his Friends in the Contentions with Sylla, he retired to Athens where he spent most of his Time in Study, and the Income of his Estate in public and private Benefactions; and became so dear to the People there, that they almost adored him; yet he would never allow them to erect so much as one Statue to his Honour, tho' it was their constant Practice to all such as deserved well of their State. From hence it was he took the Name of Atticus (or Athenian, for so the Word imports) here alluded to by Cicero.

But his Life may be read more at large in the mentioned Author Cornelius Nepos, now in English. I shall therefore only add, That he was about two Years older than Cicero, but survived him 12 Years, dying in his 78th Year, in the 722d after the Building of Rome, and about 30 Years before the Birth of our Saviour; Cicero being put to Death by M. Anthony's Order, in his 64th Year, and in the 710th of Rome. That his Sister was married to Quintus Cicero, Brother to the Author; his Daughter to the Emperor Augustus's great Friend and Favourite M. Agrippa, whose Daughter by her was the first and the beloved Wife of Augustus's Successor the Emperor Tiberius; but he was obliged to part with her, to marry his Father-in-Law Augustus's Daughter, the infamous Julia. I shall, in relation to both Cicero and Atticus, add a Sentence of Seneca's, in his 21st Epipstle to Lucilius.

> "Cicero's Epistles (says he) will not suffer Atticus's Name to die. His Son-in-Law Agrippa, his Grandson-in-Law Tiberius, or his Grand-Nephew Drufus Cæsar, would have avail'd him nothing; amongst all those great Names and Affinities he would not have been remembered, had not Cicero grafted him into his own Fame."

Yet Atticus wrote some valuable Books himself but they are all lost.

2 Ennius, born in Calabria, now Part of the Kingdom of Naples, under the Consuls Q. Valerius and A. Mamilius, in the 515th Year of Rome, as A. Gellius from Varro informs us; went to live in the Island Sardinia, to which Marcus Cato, the Speaker in this Tract, being sent Prætor, and becoming acquainted with Ennius, he there began to learn Greek of him, and on his Return brought him to Rome; which, Nepos says, was an Act of greater Importance than a

Notes for page 2

Triumph. He wrote the Annals of Rome in Verse, which, tho' highly valued by the Romans, and often quoted by Cicero are now, excepting some Fragments, intirely lost. He is more particularly mentioned again in this Discourse.

3 Titus Quinctius Flaminius, who, when Consul in the Year of Rome 556, overcame Philip the last King of that Name, and the last but one of Macedon; after which, at the great Solemnity of the Isthmian Games that then ensued, and at which there was a general Concourse from all the neighbouring Parts and Countries, he by publick Proclamation restored to the several States of Greece their ancient Liberties, after they had been deprived of them, and continued in Subjection to others, but principally to the Kings of Macedon, above 120 Years. This Conquest, with his other Actions, added greatly to the former Lustre of his Family, but it receiv'd a severe Blow from this Cato, the principal Speaker here; who, when he was Censor, by virtue of that Office degraded Titus's Brother Lucius Flaminius, who had also been Consul, and bore other high Offices, from his Place in the Senate; which is mention'd further on in this Discourse, as by Cato himself, and the whole Story is there given more particularly. [See Note 63.] His Life may be read at large amongst those of Plutarch.

4 From the late Revolution in the State, by the Usurpation of Julius Cæsar, who, without any other Right or Pretence to it, than that of the Power of his Army, the Subjects as well as himself of the Common-Wealth, instead of obeying the Senate's Order to disband, he made War on his native Country, pursued Pompey, who commanded the Army of the Senate, into Greece, and at Pharsalia in Thessaly intirely routed him; made himself, on his Return to Rome, perpetual and absolute Dictator, and became the first of the Roman Emperors. For tho' about three Years after, by the Conspiracy of Brutus, Cassius and others, in Hopes of recovering their Liberties, he was stabb'd in the Senate-House; yet his Sister Julia's Grandson Octavius, a Youth then, but of about 18 Years, whom he had by Will made his Heir, found Means to get into the same Seat, and cloath himself with the same Power; and from him it was continued (tho' only for four Successions in his own, or rather in his Wife Livia's Family, who all proved Tyrants, and two of the four, Caligula and Nero,

meer Monsters of Cruelty) till Rome itself became a Prey to the Goths, or other Northern Nations.

But on mentioning this first of the Roman Emperors, it may not be amiss here to observe of him, that tho' he was a Person of the sublimest Genius, adorned with every Accomplishment of Nature or Art, and not at all of a cruel Disposition, but on the contrary of a Temper truly clement and generous; yet by the Iniquity of the Times, he seemed to have been sent into the World for the Destruction of Mankind: For Pliny, after a most exalted Character of his Abilities [*Nat. Hist. L. 7. c. 25.*] tells us, that he himself acknowledged he had in his Wars destroyed the Lives of 1,192,000 Men, exlusive of these that fell in those horrid Civil Wars he engag'd his Country in; for which Lipsius, on mentioning this, [*De constantia Lib. 2. c. 22.*] justly calls him *Pestem perniciemque generis humani,* The Pest and Plague of Human Kind. And tho' the Numbers of those that fell in their Civil Contentions, are not mentioned, yet they may be guessed at, by comparing the two last Census taken of the Men of Rome, that are mentioned by Livy in the Epitomes of his Books still extant; for 'tis noted in that of his 98th Book, in the 682d Year of the City, that the Number was no less than 450 thousand Men, but in the Year 706, on Cæsar's Return from his Victory over Pompey, the Number was reduced to 150 thousand; so that the City of Rome alone, and chiefly by these Contentions, lost two full Thirds of her People, and she still continued to lose by the ensuing Wars after Cæsar's Death, carried on by Octavius (afterwards Augustus) and Anthony, against Brutus and Cassius, & c.

5 In what Year of his Life Cicero wrote this excellent little Tract, does not clearly appear. He was born in the 647th Year of Rome; J. Cæsar made himself Master of the Empire after his Return from Egypt in the 706th Year; after which, Cicero wrote most of his Philosophical Discourses. From his Preface to his 2d Book *de Divinatione,* we find, that this was composed after his *Academics,* his Books *de Finibus,* his *Tuscan Questions,* and those *de Natura Deorum*: And from the same and other Hints we also learn, that it was wrote before those *de Divinatione,* his Lælius or *of Friendship,* his excellent *Offices,* and his Book *de Fato*; all which we find were wrote after Cæsar's Death. [Vid. his Preface to Lælius, *de Officiis, Lib. 2.* and his Preface to that de Fato.] 'Tis therefore

Notes for page 4

probable he wrote this in the last Year of Cæsar's Life, who was murther'd on the Ides (the 15th Day) of March, *A. U. 709*, that is in Cicero's 63d Year. He was himself murther'd in his 64th Year, by Order M. Anthony, the next Year after Cæsar's Fall.

6 Tithonus was said to be the Son of Laomedon, King of Troy, of such admirable Beauty, that, according to the Fictions of the Poets, Aurora the Goddess of the Morning, fell in Love with him. And of her he obtained that he might live very long; which he did to that Degree, that wearing gradually away, he shrunk at length into a Grasshopper. The Moral of which is plain, *i.e.* That Tithonus was very comely in his Youth, an early Riser, and regular in his Life; that by these Means he attained to a great Old Age, in which he still preserved his Agility, but grew very thin, and became vastly altered from his former State, when in his Bloom.

7 Marcus Porcius Cato of which Name there were two Persons very famous in the Roman History: And the Lives of both are in Plutarch, an Author now in the Hands of most English Readers of History. But of the Eldest, who is the Person intended here by Cicero, I shall add the following Account from the great Historian Livy, whose Work is not yet so common in our Language. In Bo. 39. c. 40. speaking of the Election of Censors, in the 570th Year of the City, for which there stood six Candidates of the Nobility, and as many of the Commons, of whom Cato was one; (and he was perfectly *Novus Homo*, a New Man; so they called those of obscure Families who got Offices in the State; but new as he was, he had been Consul 11 Years before, in the 36th of his Age:) The Historian, I say, having named the 12 Candidates, proceeds thus;

> "But Marcus Porcius Cato had vastly the Advantage of them all, as well of the Patricians as the Plebeians of the greatest Families." [For there were illustrious ones of the latter as well as of the former.] "This Man (says he) was Master of such natural Abilities, and of so much Spirit, that where-ever he had been born, he would have made his Fortune. He was skill'd in every Art, both of publick and private Life, and equally in Affairs of both City and Country. Some have rose by their Knowledge in the Law, others by Eloquence, and others by their

military Atchievements: But he was so equally qualified for them all, that one would think him born to that alone, whatever it was, that he took in Hand. As a Soldier he was brave, and signalized his Courage in many Engagements; and when advanced to the highest Posts, a no less consummate General. In Peace, when consulted in Matters of Right, he shewed the highest Skill; and in pleading a Cause, no less Eloquence. Nor did this appear during his Life only, as in those whose Talents in that Way flourish and die with them; for His remain and live consecrated to Futurity in his Writings of every kind; as his extant *Orations*, as well in Defence of himself, as both for and against others, fully shew: For he gave his Adversaries Work, both by his Impeachments and his Vindications: And indeed he was rather too much engaged in Contention: Nor is it easy to say, whether the Nobility bore harder on him, or he on the Nobility: For his natural Temper, it must be owned, was somewhat of the harshest, and his Tongue of the fre-est. But then he had a Soul impenetrable to all the Allurements of Pleasure; most rigidly honest and unblemished, above courting the Favour of Men, and no less contemning Riches. For Parsimony, and for Patience in Fatigues and in Dangers, his Constitution both of Body and Mind seemed firm as Iron; and such as even Old-Age, to which all things yield, could not break or subdue: For in his 86th Year he had a publick Oration in his own Defence, which he also put in Writing; and in his 90th, he impleaded *Servius Galba* before the Commons."

Thus wrote Livy of Cato above a Hundred Years after his Death. From which Character we may observe Cicero made a most proper Choice of his Speaker, and the following Discourse will be found as justly to suit the Character. Other Particulars of his Life will occur further on; [for some of which, see Note 56, 71, 89, & c.] The Word he alludes to for his Name, is *Catus*, which signifies *circumspect, cautious, cunning*.

The other of the same Name was his Great Grandson, by his Son Marcus and Tertia, Paulus Æmilius's Daughter, both mentioned hereafter, called Cato Junior, or Uticensis from the Place of his Death; who for his Virtues gained a greater Reputation, and became more famous, even than his Ancestor; of whom

Notes for page 4

(since his Life, as I have said, is in Plutarch) I shall here only give this short Character from Vellius Paterculus, An old Roman Historian, who wrote about 75 Years after his Death; and in Book 2. chap. 35. speaks thus of him: "He was the very image of Virtue itself; in his Disposition more like a God than Man; who never did a good Thing that he might be seen to do It, but because he could not act otherwise; whose only Rule in Life was Justice; untoucht with any human Vice, and ever in himself superior to every Attack of Fortune."

I shall also further observe, that He is the principal Hero of Lucan's Pharsalia, a Poem never finished, but generally wrote with a true Spirit of Liberty, even under the Tyranny of Nero; but it cost the Author his Life. In the 9th Book of that Poem, after a most beautiful Character of that Excellent Great Man, the Poet concludes (according to the Religion of that Time, when Rome took upon it to people Heaven with Gods, as it now does with Saints to be pray'd to) with those most remarkable Lines:

*Ecce parens verus patriæ, dignissimus aris*
*Roma tuis, per quem nunquam jurare pudebit,*
*Et quem st steteris unquam cervice joluta*
*Tunc olim factura deum*

Thus Englished by N. Rowe:

*His Country's Father here, O* Rome*, behold,*
*Worthy thy Temples, Priests, and Shrines of Gold;*
*If e'er thou break thy lordly Master's Chain,*
*If Liberty be e'er restor'd again,*
*Him thou shall place in the divine Abodes,*
*Swear by his holy Name, and rank him with thy Gods.*

To avoid seeing the Subversion of the Liberties of Rome, he kill'd himself, in the 49th Year of his Age. Livy Epit. lib. 114.

8 Scipio and Lælius. There were two Pairs of illustrious Romans of these Names, noted for their mutual Friendship. The first flourished in the Time of, and acted very great Parts in the 2d Punic or Carthaginian War: For this Scipio was the Man, to whom Rome not only ow'd its own Deliverance and Safety, but nearly all her Advantages and Conquests over the Carthaginians; who, after

they had brought that City to the very Brink of Ruin, were afterwards obliged, and principally by the Conduct of Scipio, to submit to hard Conditions of Peace; [see Note 24 & 29.] For which he afterwards bore the Name of Scipio Africanus, as the Conqueror of Asric: And in all these Actions Lælius was his almost inseperable Companion.

But the Pair of the same Names here intended by Cicero, were two Generations younger. This Scipio was the real Son of the Great Paulus Æmilius, whose Life is amongst those of Plutarch, [see Note 24.] but was, after the Manner of the Romans, adopted by the Son Of the first Great Scipio Africanus; who, being himself but of a weakly Constitution of Body for a Son to succeed him, chose one of that illustrious Family of the Æmilii: Hence laying down his paternal Name, he, according to Custom, took that of the Family he was grafted into; and afterwards, for his Conquest and Demolition of Carthage in the 3d Punic War [see Note 29.] he also bore the Name of Scipio Africanus; but to distinguish him from his Grandfather, he was called Africanus Junior, and frequently from his own Father's Name, Scipio Æmilianus. He had also the Title Numantinus given him, from his Reduction, or more properly, the utter Destruction of the famous (the glorious) City of Numantia in Spain; in which, as brave a People as ever were known on Earth, and who as little deserv'd it, were utterly destroyed, Men, Women and Children; not in open Battle, nor by taking the Place by Force; for the Romans durst not engage them; but by hemming them in with greater Numbers, and utterly starving them.

Yet this Scipio was in himself a most excellent Person, and in all other Respects, save in these two inhuman Atchievements, the Destruction of Carthage and of Numantia, which were done in Obedience to the State, and were in those Times accounted glorious; he appears to have deserved the Character given him by the before-mentioned Paterculus, L. I. C. 12. which is this:

> "A Man who equall'd the Virtues of his Grandfather Scipio, and of his own Father Paulus Æmilius; who, for every Accomplishment either for the Sword or Gown [War or Peace] for his natural Abilities, and his vast Improvements of these, was undoubtedly the most eminent of his Age; who, in the whole Course of his Life, never did, spoke or thought a thing that was not worthy of Praise."

# *Notes for Chapters III and IV*

Notes for pages 8-11

But having opposed the Party of that turbuluent Tribune Caius Gracchus, Brother to his Wife Sempronia, and Grandson to the first Great Scipio Africanus before-mentioned by his admired Daughter Cornelia, and consequently this Scipio's own First-Cousin, as was shewn before, by his Adoption; after he had been waited on home in full Health by the principal Senators, he was the next Morning found dead in his Bed, strangled as some thought, or, as others, poisoned, and not without his Wife's Privity: Nor was his Death further inquired into; such was the Confusion of the Time. Thus ended that very Great Man, in the 56th Year of his Age, and in the 625th of the City. *Vell. Paterc. lib. 2. c. 4. & Liv. lib. 59. in arg. & Freinsheim Suppl.* But notwithstanding all the Opportunities he had of enriching himself, we find by Aurelius Victor, that he died but poor, as Cato also did (see Note 89.) which is a further Proof of the Integrity of both. Plutarch wrote the Lives of both these Scipio's, but they are both lost.

His Friend Lælius, was Caius Lælius, surnamed Sapiens, the Wife, who was Consul the 614th Year of the City. Cicero taking Occasion from the known Friendship between him and Scipio, makes him the chief Speaker (as Cato is here) in that other fine Discourse of his, which bears his Name LÆLIUS, on the Subject of *Friendship,* wrote afterwards, and directed to the same T. P. Atticus, with this.

## CHAPTER III

9 Salinator was Consul in the 566th Year, Albinius in the 568th, but Cato in the 559th Year of the City. See Note 17.

10 One of Seriphos, a small barren Island in the in the Ægean Sea.

## CHAPTER IV

11 Quintus Fabius Maximus, who, after the Romans had in several successive Battles been defeated at the Rivers Ticinus and Trebia, and the Thrasymene Lake, by Annibal, was in the 537th Year of Rome, appointed Dictator or absolute Commander, an Office that legally was to continue but Six Months, and for that Time abrogated the Power of the Consul and of all other

Magistrates, but that of the Tribunes of the People, and of the lower ones, necessary for administering Justice and keeping the Peace; but under him his Master of Horse had also a considerable Power. In which Time he kept Annibal at a Bay; constantly declining, however provoked, to engage with him; tho' by the Rashness of Minucius, his Master of Horse, invested with too much Power by the People, all had like to be lost again; and after he laid down, the terrible Battle of Cannæ was fought, wherein 80 Senators and 45,000 of the Roman Army fell Two Years after this, Fabius was the fourth time Consul, and after six Years more, the fifth, *An Urb.* 545.



12 In the 521st Year of Rome, 233 Years before Christ, therefore Cato was born in the 520th.

13 Twenty Years of Age.—— A Quæstor in the City was a Treasurer; in the Army he took an Account of, and received what was gain'd to the Public from the Enemy; kept Lists of the Army, and took Accounts of the Slain on both Sides. The Ædile's Business was to look after all Buildings, public and private, Weights and Measures, to order the public Games, & c. Prætors were the chief City-Magistrates in Rome, and abroad were Governors in Civil Affairs.

14 At Thirty Years.

15 When a Law was proposed, it was read publickly to the People, and then fixed up for three Nundinæ, or 27 Days; after which, the People being met, some Person of Authority (for it was not allowed to all) who approved of the Law, besides the Proposer, recommended it to the People, in a public Speech. This was called, *suadere legem,* and the Speaker, *Suasor legis,* as here this Fabius did for the Law here mentioned, the Year before he died, which was in the 551st of Rome, having (as *Liv. 1.* 30. *c.* 26. hints, but gives it not as certain) born the Office of Augur for 62 Years.

16 A Law proposed by Marcus Cincius, the Tribune, that those who pleaded Causes, should take no Fees nor Rewards.

# *Notes for Chapter IV*

Notes for page 12

17 Tarentum or Tarntus, a great City, situate to the Head of the great Bay of that Name, now Tarento, was surrender'd to the Consul Papirius, in the Year of Rome 482, two hundred seventy-two Years before Christ, after Pyrrhus had left it, but with a Garrison of Epirotes in it; of whom the City being tired, submitted to the Romans; by whom, for the abusive Treatment of their Ambassadors about nine Years before, they were then besieged. In the 2d Punic War, in the 542d Year of Rome, some Conspirators in the City, incensed at their Hostages being put to Death in Rome, for attempting to make their Escape, betrayed it to Annibal: Which was very much owing to the Negligence of Salinator, then Governor of it. Livy, Bo. 25. tells the Story particularly, without mentioning or blaming the Governor, whom he does not name; sparing him probably in regard to his Family: But Polybius, in the *Excerpta* we have of his 8th Book, is much more particular, and says he was drunk the Evening of the Night it was taken.

For this Reason it is, probably, and because Spurius Albinus had gained so ill a Character for his Conduct in the Army, that Cicero makes Cato mention these two particularly, to their Disadvantage. The Words which Cato here says he heard Salinator himself utter, Plutarch in Cato's Life says were spoke in the Senate: He doubtless meant, that if he had not defended the Castle (which he did bravely enough) Fabius could not have recovered the Town. But that does not at all appear: It was regained much as it was lost, *viz* by Treachery, but of a meaner sort; for it was betray'd by its Governor's Love to a young Woman in the City, that had a Brother in the Roman Army, who under Fabius laid the Plot. Annibal was the Contriver of the first Delivery, and Fabius of the second; upon the News of which Annibal only dropt this Expression, "Well (says he) I see the Romans have also their Annibals." See Livy Bo. 27. and Plutarch in the Life of Fabius.

18 The second Decad of Livy being lost, this I think is no where else mentioned.

19 The Romans were so exceedingly superstitious, that they would undertake nothing of Moment without some previous Divination. For this they had Augurs Auspices and Aruspices appointed. The Augurs were the Chief, of whom there was a College, consisting at first, by Romulus's Institution, of only

three, but afterwards gradually increased to nine, and under the Emperors, to fifteen. Their Business was to pronounce good or ill Luck from the Flight or Chirping or Noise of Birds; the Feeding of Chickens kept for that Purpose, &c. For most gross Instances of this Superstition of theirs, see Plutarch in the Life of Marcellus, near the Beginning.

20 The Dead Bodies of the Romans were commonly burnt in a Funeral Pile, at which the nearest Friend of the Deceased, if of Note, made a Funeral Oration, which was generally a Panegyric on the Deceased and his Family.

## CHAPTER V

21 Isocrates was Contemporary with Socrates, Plato, &c. at Athens: He taught Rhetoric or Oratory in a private School, and many of the greatest Men of the Age, were his Scholars. This Panathenaic is one of his Orations, which we have yet extant; It is by much the longest of them all; the Subject is, the Commendation of his Countrymen the Athenians, and to prove their Merit, in respect to the rest of Greece, was greater than that of the Lacedemonians: Towards the End of it he says, He then wanted but three Years of a Hundred: Of which 'tis strange, that neither his Commentator Wolfius nor Fabricius have taken any Notice, tho' they both quote this Passage of Cicero for his Age. [See Note 43d towards the End.] Philostratus says, he died of Grief, on hearing the Athenians had lost the Battle of Chæronea. (Which was fought against Philip of Macedon, Olympiad. 110. 3. the 415th Year of Rome.)

Gorgias was of Leontium in Sicily; he went about the Cities of Greece, teaching the young Men Oratory, and the Philosophy of that Time, for very high Pay. He is said to have been the first who offered to speak *extemporé*, to any Subject that should be proposed to him. He was much honoured, tho' Plato in a Dialogue that bears his Name, exposes him for his Presumption. His Statue was erected of Gold in the Pythian Temple: Pliny, *lib.* 33. *c.* 4. says, by himself, and at his own Charge; but Philostratus, Cicero, *de Orat. lib.* 3. and others, say, it was done by the Publick. Pliny adds, that it was erected in the 70th Olympiad, *i.e.* about the 254th Year of Rome.

# Notes for Chapters V and VI

Notes for pages 15-16

22 By many Passages in Cicero, and others of the Ancients, we find Strength of Sides as well as Voice, was absolutely required in an Orator; for they very properly used the Word *Sides*, as we do *Lungs*: I say, *very properly*, because the Lungs have in themselves no manner of Force; but their whole Motion depends on the Muscles of the Sides and Breast.

23 The Voconian Law was, that no Woman should enjoy by Will, more than one Fourth Part of an Estate of a full Rate or Cense, that is, of 100,000 Sesterces, which is about 800 Pounds Sterling.

## CHAPTER VI

24 Lucius Paulus Æmilius had by his first Wife Papiria, two Sons and two Daughters mention'd in History; and putting her away (without assigning any other Reason for it, than Julius Cæsar on the like Occasion did afterwards, by holding out his new Shoe, and asking if it was not handsome, but did they know where it pinch'd him?) he married a second; he also gave away these two Sons, to be adopted (after the Roman Manner) into other Families: The younger was adopted by Scipio, the Son of the Great Publius Cornelius Scipio Africanus before-mentioned, and is the Person here spoke to. [See Note 8.] The other Son of Paulus was adopted into the Family of Fabius Maximus, and became also famous: One of the Daughters, named Tertia, was married to Cato's Son Marcus here mentioned [see Note 89] who died a few Years before; the other Daughter was married to one of the Tubero's, of a very poor, but virtuous Family. [See Plutarch in Paulus Æmilius.] He lost two Sons just at the time of his Triumph over Perseus, King of Macedon; both of them by his second Marriage, the one of fourteen Years, five Days before the Triumph, and the other of twelve Years, within three Days after it; so that he had none left to succeed him in Name, or in his own Family.

He was in all things a great Man in himself, but unhappily the Minister of the Senate's Severity, in executing their Commands upon the Epirotes, for joining with Perseus, after they had submitted to Rome. For his Army in one Day plunder'd 70 of their Towns, and took 150,000 Captives, whom they sold for Slaves; and from the Prey each Horseman had (as Livy says, *lib.* 45. *c.* 34.) four hundred Denarij, about £.12. 10. Sterling, and each Footman half as

much. 'Tis therefore strange that Plutarch (in Paul. Æmil.) should say, they had but eleven Denarij, or about 6 Shill. 10½ d. each. But into the Publick Treasury he brought 135,000 lb. Weight of Silver, and 13,860 Pound of Gold, all carried in Baskets before him, with other vast Riches besides, in his Triumph, which was exceeding splendid.

25 Caius Fabricius Luscinius, with the others here named, were all famous in the Time of the War with Pyrrhus; the Time when Rome seemed to be at its Heighth of Glory for Virtue; tho' they were much more so afterwards for Conquest and Empire. Fabricius was Consul twice, *viz.* in the 472d, and 476th Years of Rome, and he triumphed twice: Pyrrhus landing with Forces in Italy to assist the Farentines against the Romans, gained the first Battle against the Consul Albinius; but being convinced, in that Engagement, of the Roman Bravery, he was rather desirous, upon his victory, to make an honourable Peace for himself, and a safe one for his Allies of Italy, than to prosecute the War. Fabricius being sent to redeem the Roman Captives, was treated with the utmost Civility by Pyrrhus, who pressed him (being known to be very poor) to accept of a Present of Gold, as a Token of Friendship only; but he obstinately refused it: The next Day he endeavor'd to terrify him with an Elephant, but in vain. Pyrrhus gave 200 Captives their Freedom without Redemption: To the rest (about 1600) he gave Liberty to go home to keep their *Saturnalia* (Festivals kept in December, like the modern Christmas) on Fabricius's Word that they should return, if Peace were not made, or they were not redeemed; which they did punctually at the Day.

When Censor, he was very severe, and turn'd Rufinus (a Man of great Merit, who had been twice Consul and Dictator, and had triumphed) out of the Senate; for no other Crime, than that he had Ten Pounds of Silver-Plate in his House; a Piece (as was then judged) of intolerable Luxury; on which Val. Max. (*lib. 2. c. 9.*) is pleasant: And this is mention'd in Livy's Epit. *lib.* 14. Yet Fabricius had a small Silver Salt, and a little Silver Cup with a Horn Foot to it, which he had received of his Ancestors, and kept for his Libations or Sacrifices. On his Return from Pyrrhus, he was first made Lieutenant to the Consuls, and the next Year Consul; being then General, Pyrrhus's Physician (whom Plutarch calls Timochares, others Nicias) coming into the Roman Camp, offered to Fabricius for a suitable Reward to poison Pyrrhus; which he heard with

Detestation, and (as Plutarch, in Pyrrhus's Life, relates it) revealed it directly to Pyrrhus, in a very handsome Letter, which he gives there; but by others 'tis told variously, tho' all agree in the Substance of the Story.

26 Manius Curius Dentatus was thrice Consul. In the Fasti he is mark'd as if he had been four times, but it does not appear he was more than thrice. His first Consulate was in the 464th Year of Rome, and he then triumphed twice in the same Year, *viz.* over the Samnites and the Sabines. The second time [mark'd the 3d] was in the Year 479, fifteen Years after the first; he then fought with and intirely routed Pyrrhus after his Return from Sicily to Italy; upon which Pyrrhus abandon'd his new Allies, quitted Italy, and fail'd to his own Country Epirus, leaving only a Garrison in Tarentum; and Curius led a Triumph for his Victory. Curius was made Consul again the next Year, to oppose Pyrrhus, in case he should return, as he pretended to the Tarentines. He had most of the Glory of this War.

But he was no less famous for his great Modesty, and contented Poverty; of which an Instance is given in this Discourse, in ch. 16. His Farm, on which he lived and wholly depended, consisted only of seven Roman Jugera, or about four English Acres and an half, as others in that Neighbourhood then did; and being offered more by the Senate, he refused it, saying (as Pliny, *lib.* 18. *c.* 3. has it) that he was a dangerous Citizen [*perniciosus civis*] whom seven Jugera could not suffice; for (he adds) that was the Quantity assigned to the Commons, after the expulsion of the Kings.

27 Titus Coruncanius was Consul in the 474th Year of Rome, the first Year that Pyrrhus attack'd and beat the Romans: But he was not in the Battle himself, but at the Head of another Army warring with the Tuscans, whom he vanquished, and had a Triumph for it.

28 Appius Claudius Cæcus was Consul in the 446th Year of Rome, and again in the 457th. In the 473d Year he was carried to the Senate in a Chair on that Occasion, having, because of his Blindness, left it for many Years. His Speech is in Plutarch, in the Life of Pyrrhus. He is mention'd again, in Ch. xi.

# Notes for Chapter VI

Notes for page 18

29 Carthage ('tis said) was built by Dido from Tyre, about 70 Years before Rome. Both these Cities increasing vastly in Strength and Power, became jealous of each other. Their first War began in the 490th Year of Rome; 264 before Christ, and continued 23 Years: The Carthaginians being worsted in this long and bloody War, were on the Peace obliged to pay the Romans a yearly Tribute Of 1200 Talents [about 225,000 £. Sterl.] and to give up all their Claim to the Islands between Italy and Afric, as Sicily, Sardinia, &c. Tired with this Tribute 24 Years after the Peace, at the Instances of Annibal, a second War was commenced, in which that General led an Army of 100,000 Foot and Horse, from Spain thro' Gaul into Italy; and gaining many great Battles, and over-running the whole Country, had nearly put an End to Rome.

In Spain also the two Scipio's, endeavouring to prevent Hasdrubal from marching to join Annibal in Italy, were with their Armies cut to Pieces, [see Note 97.] after which none caring to venture thither, Publius Cornelius Scipio, mention'd before at Note 7, Son of Publius one of those Scipio's, and Nephew to the other, being then but 24 Years of Age, offered himself; and transporting some few Forces over thither, with the few scattered Remains of the Romans, which he collected, he had in five Years Time such Success, that he not only intirely defeated Hasdrubal, but expelled all the Carthaginians from Spain: He then proposed to transport the Army into Afric, to draw Annibal out of Italy; but the Senate, thinking the Attempt too desperate, would not furnish him either with Men or Money for the Expedition; Upon which, borrowing Money on his private Credit, and perswading many who admired his Virtues to accompany him, he made up a small Army of Volunteers, sailed over to Afric, there gained over to the Roman Interest Masinissa, a King in Afric, who continued faithful to the Romans above 60 Years; and had such vast Success, that Annibal with his Forces was obliged to quit Italy, and hasten home to save his own Country; but there he was also intirely defeated.

The Carthaginians, as they had begun before this Battle to sue for Peace, on the Loss of it submitted to the hard Terms the Senate of Rome imposed on them, in the 17th Year after this second War began. But the City flourishing in Trade, and still growing in Wealth and Power, gave some of Rome perpetual Apprehensions, lest some Turn of Fortune might enable them to be even with Rome again: Amongst whom this Cato was the principal; but he was opposed in

his Endeavours, to bring the Senate to a Resolution to destroy the Place, by Scipio Nasica, and many others; who look'd farther before them, and seemed to foresee, that when-ever all Danger from that Rival Power should be intirely removed, and Rome should have none capable of giving them any further Jealousy or Fear, all Discipline would be lost, Vice and Luxury would prevail, and, as it truly prov'd, introduce such Seditions, as would at length utterly sink and ruin their whole Liberties.

However 53 Years after the last Peace, in the 605th Year Of the City, a third War was declared against Carthage, on Pretence of their disturbing that near Ally and good Friend of Rome, Masinissa. The Carthaginians made the humblest Submissions to divert it; they delivered three hundred Hostages, and all their Arms, to obtain Peace: After which they received the Terms from the Senate; one of which being that Carthage itself should be demolished and razed to the Ground, and that they should not build again within less than ten Miles of the Sea. The People enraged at this, resolved rather all to lose their Lives, and die in their native Place. With the deepest Indignation therefore, and in a Fury, they set to make themselves new Arms; they cast up new Works; built Ships, and gave the Romans their Hands full for three Years. But this Scipio, having in the 2d Year of it been sent Commander against them, took and destroyed the Place, the 4th Year after the War began, which was about 5 Years after this is supposed to have been spoke to Scipio.

30 Cneius Nævius, one of the first Dramatic Writers of Rome, bore Arms in the first Punic War, and exhibited his first Piece in the 519th Year of the City. *A. Gell. lib.* 17. *c.* 21.

## CHAPTER VII

31 Themistocles, the brave Athenian General, who in the first of the 75th Olympiad, defeated Xerxes's vast Fleet at Salamis, 480 Years before Christ. Nine Years after which, the Athenians banished him. One offering to teach him the Art of Memory, he said, He would rather he should teach him that of Forgetting. His Life is among those of Plutarch.

32 Sophocles of Athens, a famous Tragic Poet, is allowed by all to have lived to

a great Age, but Authors do not agree in the Length of it. Some say, he died at 83; but I think, without good Grounds. The Author of his Life, prefix'd in Greek to the *Scholia* on him, says he was born the 2d Year of the 71st Olympiad [the 495th Year before Christ] 15 Years before the Birth of Euripides, whom he also survived (he says) six Years. That Euripides lived seventy-five Years, is particularly proved by J. Barnes in his Life. By which Account, Sophocles must have lived ninety-six Years. This Story is also in Lucian, in his *Macrobij*, or Long-livers, who says, Sophocles was choak'd with a Grape-stone, at the Age of 95 Years; that the Judges admired the Work, and condemned his Son Jophon (who was also a Tragic Writer) of Madness. Sophocles is said to have wrote 123 Tragedies, of which we yet have most of the Names; but no more than seven of the Pieces themselves left, amongst which this, called Oedipus Coloneus, is still extant.

33 Designing in these Notes to give the Ages of all the long-lived Persons here mentioned by Cicero, as far as they can be found in the ancient Writings now extant, or in others that I have; I must observe, That 'tis impossible to make so much as a rational Conjecture of the Age of him he first names after Sophocles, *viz.* Hesiod; nor (I dare venture to say) did Cicero himself know any thing certain of it, further than that, by what Hesiod says of himself, in his Piece called *Works and Days*, it appears he was an Old Man. Some have believed he lived before Homer; many that they were Contemporaries; and others, that Hesiod was considerably younger; amongst whom was Cicero himself, as he shews further on in this Piece; or probably Cato might have wrote so in his Origines. Varro, a great Antiquary of Rome, Contemporary with Cicero, fixed Homer's Age at about 160 Years after the Taking of Troy. Eusebius and Tatian reckon up many other different Opinions. H. Dodwell, our late Antiquary, a Man of vast Industry and great Penetration in these Studies, brings it about 350 Years lower, or to the 30th Olympiad, that is about 660 Years before Christ.

34 Simonides of the Island Ceos, a famous Poet, who wrote much; but nothing of his is now extant, except some Epigrams in the *Anthologia*, and a few Fragments. Plato calls him a divine Man. This is he who answered Hiero the Elder of Syracuse, inquiring of him, what God was, in the well known Manner,

Notes for page 21

mention'd by Cicero, *de nat. Deorum, lib.* I. that is, First taking one Day to consider of it, he then took two, and then four, still doubling the Time; for which he gave this Reason, that the more he thought of it, the more Time he wanted. He was born in the 55th, and died in the 78th Olympiad, aged above ninety Years.

35 Stesichorus of Sicily, a Poet much older than Simonides, was born in the 35th Olympiad, about 640 Years before Christ; he was Contemporary with Phalaris, Tyrant of Agrigentum; divers of whose Epistles, or of those now extant, called the Epistles of Phalaris, are directed to him, menacing him highly for the Opposition he truly made to him; tho' those Epistles themselves are judged not to be genuine. Suidas says, Stesichorus wrote 26 Books of Poems, in the Doric Dialect; but nothing of his is extant. Lucian says, he died aged 86 Years.

36 None doubt Homer lived to a good Age; but none can pretend to say what that was. Herodotus has left a small Piece, called Homer's Life, in which he is as particular in what the People of the several Towns and Places where Homer (as he says) had been, as if it had not been 50 Years since he was there; and yet he says his Birth was 622 Years before Xerxes passed the Hellespont into Greece, which was in the 74th Olympiad; and from hence probably Varro's Computation, which is the same with this, was taken: He also gives a particular Account of the Manner of his Death, [as he pretends] but says not a Word at what Age.

37 Pythagoras was of the Island Samos; but some believed, tho' born there, he was of a Phœnician Extract. Authors also very much differ about the Time of his Birth, and particularly three late great ones of our own Country, *viz.* Bishop Lloyd, Dr. Bently, and H. Dodwell. It is however a settled Point amongst them, that he was not born before the last Year of the 43d Olympiad, nor after the last Year of the 52d; that is, that he was born between the 604th and the 568th Years before Christ, From Samos he went over to Phœnicia; thence into Egypt, where he conversed much with their Priests; thence he went into Chaldea, and to Babylon, where some think he might have seen the Prophet Daniel.

# Notes for Chapter VII

Notes for page 21

After about 22 Years spent in these Travels, he returned to Samos, where finding the Government ursurped by Solyson, a Tyrant, he went to Lucania in Italy, where he was highly esteemed; being, by those of Metapontum, accounted a God. He had many Followers; but not admitting all that came to him, he particularly disgusted one Cylon of Croton, a young Man of great Wealth and Power, to that Degree, that by a formal Conspiracy, all his Scholars were barbarously murthered, except two, of whom Lysis was one. Porphyry wrote his Life, of which we have a large Fragment; Jamblichus more fully, both in Greek, which we also have. It is also in Diogenes Lærtius, and in Stanly's Lives of the Philosophers, with a particular Account of his Doctrine. M. Dacier has wrote it more elegantly, prefixed to his Translation of the Golden Verses, and of Hierocles's excellent Commentaries upon them; all now translated into English.

Pythagoras's Doctrine was certainly excellent; it rendred all those who adhered to it, highly virtuous, and most useful Men: But this ought to be remembred, that tho' many have pretended to give some Account of it, yet we have nothing of it truly certain; for neither himself, nor his Followers, would ever publish any thing: Only there are some few Epistles of theirs, that are accounted genuine; but chiefly on moral Duties. And the Golden Verses, so called truly, shew both what these and the Men themselves were. But many Things delivered by others, as the Opinion of that Sect, are to be suspected for fabulous: And it is to be doubted whether any Sect was ever more belyed and abused: Pythagoras is said by Jerome [that is, by Eusebius] to have died in the 70th Olympiad, at the Age Of 95, or, as others say, 75; so it is in Eusebius's Greek Text, as published by Scaliger, Pag. 166. Jerome in his Version gives only the Olympiad, not his Age. Diog. Lærtius quotes Heraclides, giving him 80; but others, he says, allow him 90 Years: And the great Is. Casaubon on the Place, thinks it ought to be 99, because Tzetzes, who generally copies from Lærtius, has it so. An anonymous Writer of his Life, of which we have an Account in *Photius, Cod.* 259, gives him 104 Years; and a medical Author, cited by Menagius on Lærtius, allows him 117 Years: So that there are no less than 42 Years Difference between the lowest and highest.

38 Democritus of Abdera, a City in Thrace, has been accounted, by many, the Author of the Atomical Philosophy, on which Epicurus afterwards built: But it

is a Mistake; for, as Dr. Cudworth, Vossius, and others shew, it was much more ancient: And Cicero, *de Nat. Deor. lib.* I. mentions Leucippus as prior to him in that Doctrine. He was contemporary with Socrates and Plato, but kept himself a Stranger to Athens; having, as some say, never seen it. He seems to have seen further into Nature, than any other Philosopher of his Age; but all his own Writings are lost, save some Citations in *Stobæus,* with some few others. But divers Things are extant under his Name, of which none are genuine, as of Chemistry, Charms, &c. Fabricius has also, in his *Biblioth. Gr.* Vol. 4, published a Fragment upon Sympathy and Antipathy in Greek, said to be lately discovered in a Library in Italy, as a genuine Piece of Democritus's; but, in my Opinion, it not only discovers itself by its Silliness, but by the Words, *O mighty Emperor,* which occur about the midst of it: It therefore seems rather to have been wrote under some of the Roman Emperors much later; unless it was adressed to the King of Persia, which is not altogether improbable; for Thrace submitted to those Monarchs, and Democritus's Father entertain'd Xerxes himself when there: But further, it is wrote in the common, and not in the Ionic Dialect, as all others of Democritus's Writings were.

And of the same kind we have divers little Pieces under the same Name, in the Collection of Greek *Geoponics,* or Husbandry, which were never wrote by this Democritus, tho' some perhaps might by another of the Name. He was so intent on Discoveries in Nature, that he said, he would prefer one to the Crown of Persia. He travelled into Egypt, and over many Parts of Asia, in quest of Knowledge; and continued very much abroad, till he was 80 Years old; then retiring and confining himself much, he applied himself to the Dissection of Animals, and to consider the minute Parts of their dead Bodies. The City of Abdera hereupon thinking him mad, and having a great Value for him, sent unknown to him an Embassy to the great Physician Hippocrates, to come to cure him. He came at their Call, tho' it was no very small Voyage; and after some Discourse with Democritus, declared to the People, That he was the only Man he found truly in his Senses in the Place.

There is extant a long and pleasant Letter of Hippocrates amongst his Works, giving a particular Narrative of the whole Affair, tho' some of late, and others formerly, suspected whether it be genuine. Democritus thought all the Cares of Life Folly, and therefore always laughed at them. Plato had such an

Abhorrence of his Corpuscular Philosophy, tho' it is now allowed on all hands to be the only true, that he has never so much as once mentioned him in his Writings. Lærtius and Lucian agree, that he lived to the Age of 104 Years: And Censorinus says, he lived to near the Age of Gorgias, which was noted before to be 108 or 107. Democtritus used to say, To advise well, to speak well, and to act well, were the three great Points Men should study.

39 Plato's Character is so well known, that much need not be said of him. Dacier has largely wrote his Life, and prefix'd it to his French Version of the Select Dialogues, published in 2 Vols. since done into English. I shall briefly observe, that he was the Son of Aristo, born at Athens the 3d Year of the 87th Olympiad, 430 Years before Christ. He applied himself in his Youth to the genteeler Exercises, as Athletics, Painting, Music and Poetry; in which last we have some small Things of his that are good. He also served in the Wars, at 20 Years of Age: But quitting all these, on observing the solid Wisdom of Socrates, he gave himself intirely up to him. Ælian (*Var. Hist. lib.* 3. 27.) says, that the Night before Plato's Father came to recommend his Son to Socrates's Care, he (Socrates) dreamed, that a young Swan flew from the Altar in the Academy, dedicated to Cupid, into his Bosom, and from thence flew up to the Heavens, singing so sweetly, as to charm both Men and Gods. He travelled into Egypt, and then to Italy, to see Archytas the Pythagorean, as is mentioned in this Piece of Cato, and to converse with others of that Sect. He was thrice in Sicily, chiefly on Dion's Account. 'Tis agreed he died in the 81st or 82d Year of his Age. The Christian Fathers admired him much. *Vld. Aug. de Civ. Dei, lib.* 8. c. 4, & *seq.*

40 Socrates his Character is also well known. M. Charpentier, one of the first Members of the French Academy, has excellently wrote his Life; which is in English prefixed to Byshe's Translation of Xenophon's 4 Books of the Memorable Things of Socrates, with his 5th of Oeconomics. He was born the 3d Year of the 77th Olympiad, and condemned and put to Death the 1st of the 95th Olympiad; aged 70 Years. He never wrote any thing that was published; but Plato made him one of the Interlocutors in most of his Dialogues.

# Notes for Chapter VII

Notes for page 21

41 Zeno was of Cittium, in the Island Cyprus. He followed Merchandize in his Youth, and coming to Athens with a Cargo of Purple and other Phœnician Goods, he lost his Ship and all on board, but saved himself. Going on shoar, he went into a Bookseller's Shop, where hearing the Man reading some Pieces of Xenophon, he asked whether and where any such Men were then to be found; (Crates happening at that time to be passing the Shop) Yes, says the Man, there goes one of them, pointing to Crates: Zeno immediately followed and accosted him, and from that Day became his Disciple. He plied his Studies exceeding close, gained great Repute, and was the Founder of the Sect of Stoics, so called from *Stoa,* a Portico in which their Lectures were held. He wrote many Books, but they are all lost. He said, the best Voyage he had ever made, was that in which he had lost all.

If he died (as Eusebius says *Gr. Chron.* p. 182) the 1st of the 129th Olympiad, he must have been born the 3d of the 109th, i.e. 342 Years before Christ; for he lived 98 Years, as both Lærtius and Lucian say, in perfect Health; and then stumbling as he went out of the Door of his School, in the Words of a Greek Verse he said aloud, *Why do you call, I come*: Upon which he went home, abstain'd from Food and died; and was succeeded in the School by the following.

42 Cleanthes of Assus in Lysia in Asia Minor, came to Athens exceeding poor, having only four Drachmas (about 2s6 Sterl.) in his Pocket: There hearing Zeno discourse, he applied himself wholly to him. To maintain himself, having attended in the School all the Day, he wrought at Nights in drawing Water for the Gardens, and in grinding or bolting for the Baker; and keeping himself hearty and in good Case, while he was not observed to do any thing in the Day, and was known to have no Estate, he was called on by Areopagus (a great Court at Athens) to render them (according to an excellent Law of theirs) an Account how he lived; which he did by calling the Gardiner and Baker, for whom he wrought, to witness for him. The Court were so pleased with this, that they ordered ten Minæ (about £. 31. 5. Sterl.) of the publick Money to be given him, which his Master Zeno perswaded him not to accept. But Antigonus, King of Macedon, afterwards gave him much more. He used to pick up dry Shoulder-blade Bones of Oxen, to take down his Master's Lectures on, for want of Paper, or of the other Materials then in Use for Writing. He succeeded Zeno in his School, and grew into very high Esteem with the Athenians.

# Notes for Chapter VII

Notes for page 21

He lived to the Age of 99 Years; then having a Swelling rise on his Lip, and being ordered by the Physicians to fast two Days, in order to abate the Humour; having done so, he began to consider, what further Business he had in Life; and thereupon resolved, since he had begun to fast, he would eat no more at all; but receiving that Day a Letter from a distant Friend, requesting a Piece of Service of him, he eat enough to enable him to go abroad and do that Business; which having dispatch'd, he return'd, wholly abstain'd from Food, and died.

43 Diogenes, called the Babylonian, is mention'd by Cicero in divers Places of his Works. He was a Hearer of Chrysippus, who succeeded Cleanthes before mention'd, and the next in that School. The Succession was thus:

*The Old or First Academics,*
1. Plato, 2. Speusippus, 3. Xenocrates, 4. Polemo,
5. Crates and Crantor, carried on the Academic School.
*Stoics,*
Under Crates sprung,
6. Zeno, 7. Cleanthes, 8. Chrysippus, 9. Diogenes.

This Diogenes, together with Carneades the Academic (of the 2d School) and Critolaus the Peripatetic, were sent jointly by the City of Athens (in the 599th Year of Rome, or 155 Years before Christ) to the Senate to beg off a Fine of 500 Talents [93,750 £. Sterl.] laid on them, upon the Complaint of the Oropians, or at least a Mitigation of it. The Youth of Rome hearing them, especially Carneades speak, were so taken with their Eloquence, that they applied themselves with the utmost Eagerness to the Study of it. Cato observing this, tho' he must then have learned Greek himself, being about 80 Years of Age, and apprehending the Consequence, if the Youth declining the severer Institutions of their Ancestors, should run into the Novelties, and study the Arts of Greece, prevailed with the Senate to send those Gentlemen a going; which they did, with a favourable Answer, remitting, as some say, four Fifths of the Fine. [See *Plutarch in Cato,* and *Suppl. Livij, lib.* 47. 25.] I find this Diogenes's Age mention'd by none but Lucian, who says he died at 89 Years. *Aul. Gellius, lib.* 7. 14, *Macrobius Sat. lib.* 1. 51 *Seneca de Ira, lib.* 3. all mention these three.

Notes for pages 22-24

In closing this Account of Old Men, I shall add, That 'tis strange Cicero should omit naming a Person he so much admired, as Theophrastus; who says, in the Preface of his Characters of Vices, that he wrote them in the 99th Year of his Age: And Jerome, *in Epist.* 2. *ad Nepotianum*, says, he lived to 107 Years, and then complain'd he must die just as he began to be wise. I shall wind up this whole Account of Long-livers, by observing, That not-withstanding it has been said of divers of them, that tho' they had wrote much, all their Books were now lost; yet there are still extant three Greek Pieces, all wrote by Persons living in the same City (Athens) and in the same Age, each of whose Authors was, at the Time of writing them, above 90 Years old, and two of them, *viz.* the two last, near a hundred; these are Isocrates's Panathenaicus, and Sophocles's Tragedy of Oedipus Coloneus, both mention'd before, and that which I just now noted, Theophrastus's Characters, translated of late Years into most, if not all, the politer European Languages. And the Reason why nothing like this has appear'd in these latter Ages, may deserve to be inquired into, and considered. But the Observation I thought proper for this Place.

44 Statius Cæcilius, a Poet of Rome, but an Insubrian, or of Cisalpine Gaul by Birth, was Contemporary with Ennius, and died the next Year after him. Cicero, or Cato, calls him here by both Names, but both note the same Man. *Vossius de Poetis Lat.* These Quotations being from Comedy, are not truly in Verse, and therefore not in Rhyme here.

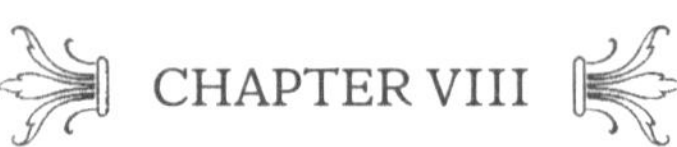

## CHAPTER VIII

45 Solon, one of those seven, called the Wise-Man of Greece, was Archon or Prætor of Athens, the 3d of the 46th Olympiad, 594 Years before Christ; and having done many great Services for that Republick (tho' he was himself a Native of Salamis, an Island not far from Athens) the People would have given him the absolute Command, but he refused it. [*Diog. Lært.*] At Athens as formerly at Rome, Debtors who could not pay, were made Servants or Slaves to the Creditors; Solon having 7 Talents [£. 1312. 10. Sterl.] due to him, remitted it, and caused all the Citizens in the same Manner to remit their Debts. The City at that Time had only Draco's Laws, said (because of their Severity) to be wrote in Blood: These he abolish'd, and gave the People new ones, many of which were excellent.

He foretold Pisistratus's Usurpation, but was not believed: When that Man got Possession of the Government, Solon went to Cræsus, King of Lydia; his Conversation with whom is well known: Pisistratus proved moderate in his Government, and invited Solon back, but he declined to come. He wrote many Elegies, some Fragments of which are extant. He died in Cyprus, at 80 Years of Age; Lucian says 100: His Body was by his Order carried to Salamis, and buried in a Corn-Field, which he required to be plowed over him. See further, Note 92.

## CHAPTER IX

46 Milo, of Croton, a City of the Brutij in the South of Italy, now in the Kingdom of Naples, was six times Victor at the Olympic Games. Divers odd Stories are told of his great Strength, as that he carried a large Ox on his Shoulders, thro' the whole Olympic Field, as if it had been a Lamb: It is commonly added, That he began with carrying a Calf, and, continuing that Practice every Day with the same Creature, till it grew to its full Size, gained Strength by it. Whence the Proverb,

*Tauruns feret, qui vitulum tulit;*
*He'll carry an Ox, that begins with a Calf;*

which sometimes is interpreted to another Sense. What Solinus tells of him, is much stranger, That with a Blow of his Fist he fell'd an Ox, and eat him all up the same Day. Aul. Gellius. *l.* 17. *c.* 16. gives this Account of his Death, That seeing a Tree split down in Part, to try what Strength he had left, he attempted to rive it quite asunder; and when he had forced it in Part, the Tree recovering itself, bound his Hands in the Rift, and held him, being alone and without Help, till he perish'd.

But the Story Diodorus Siculus gives us, in which this Milo was concerned, is much more worthy of Notice. Sybaris was a wealthy populous City, in the Borders of Lucania and the Brutij, and had divers others subject to it: The Faction of one Telys (a Citizen of great Power) prevailing, 500 of the principal Inhabitants were banished by him, and their Estates confiscated. These fled to Croton, and to the Altars there for Refuge. Telys on hearing this, by a Message required the Crotoniates to surrender them, or otherwise they might expect a War. The Crotoniates long doubtful what to do, were prevailed on by Pythagoras, then present, rather to depend on the Assistance of the Gods, and hazard a War, than betray their Supplicants. The Sybarites hereupon brought an Army of 300,000 Men into the Field; the Crotoniates met them with 100,000, with Milo at their Head; fought the Sybarites, beat them, and, giving no Quarter, cut almost the whole Army in the Battle and Flight to Pieces; and utterly destroying the Town, put an End to their whole Dominion: So that Sybaris was no more heard of, but in Story, by that Name; for Thetrium was built by the Athenians in its Place. Strabo, an excellent Geographer, under the Reign of Augustus Cæsar, who, as well as Diodorus, relates this, says, That these two Towns were but 200 Stadia, i.e. 25 Miles, distant from each other. —— The Action must have happen'd near the 50th Olympiad, and about 600 Years before Christ.

This was not necessary for illustrating Cicero; but my Design in relating it, is to note the vast Populousness of some Countries in former Ages. 'Tis true, that in those Times, War was not carried on by Mercenaries, as now; but every Man from 16 to 60 was obliged to bear Arms. Many other astonishing Instances may be given, of the vast Numbers of People in those Times in Italy, Greece, Sicily, Egypt, Asia, &c. But no-where more than in the Old Testament, where it is said [2 *Chron. c.* 13.] that Abijah led an Army of 400,000 Men against Jeroboam, who met him with another of 800,000, and that 500,000 of the latter fell in the Battle; yet their two Cities were not 50 Miles distant from each other, nor their whole Dominions, taken together; much above thrice the Extent of Yorkshire.

47 I find no Sextus Æmilius in the Roman History; perhaps it should be *M. Æmilius*, that is Marcus Æmilius Lepidus, who was Consul the first time in the 567th Year of the City, and was also Pontifex Maximus, Prince of the Senate, and Censor; and died old, in the Year of Rome 602, about a Year or two before this Discourse was held or supposed; for by Cato's being in his 84th Year, as he says, that would fall in the 603d of Rome. But the various Readings give L. Ælius, one perhaps of that poor, but excellent Family of the Ælij Tuberones, into which P. Æmilius's second Daughter was married, as was observed in Note 24.

# Notes for Chapter IX



48 Mention'd before in Note 27.

49 Publius Licinius Crassus I suppose, who was Consul in the Year 583; or rather his Father, of the same Name, who was Consul in the 549th Year, and bore all the other great Offices, as Pont. Max. and Censor; and died in the 571st of Rome. *Livy, lib.* 42. *c.* 28 & *lib.* 39. *c.* 46.

50 See Note 97.

51 See Note 24.

52 See Note 7 and 29.

53 Lucius Cæcilius Metellus was the first time Consul in the 502d Year of Rome, 250 Years before Christ, when, commanding in Sicily in the first Punic War, he defeated Asdrubal the Carthaginian General, kill'd 20,000 of his Men, with 26 Elephants, and took above a hundred, which he presented to Rome for a Show. *Eutrop. lib.* 2. He was second time Consul in 507; and, by what is said here, he must have been made Pontifex in 511, and have lived to 533, at which Time Cato must have been only 14 Years old.

54 Pontifex Maximus. The Romans, tho' they did not practise all the little Fopperies of the Greeks in their Religion, as Diod. Siculus notes; yet not only the People, but the Government itself, were as superstitious as any in the World; as was observed at Note 19: Which was principally owing to the solemn Institutions of their second King, Numa Pompilius, who, during his long Reign of 43 Years, applied himself to little besides. He appointed an Order of Priesthood, of which he made 4 Chief Pontiffs, who took their Titles [as Plutarch and Varro say] from their having the Charge of their great wooden Bridge over Tiber: These were afterwards increased to 9, and again to 15: They were chosen out of the greatest Men of Rome for Authority in the State; they held their Offices for Life; the Succession was by Election, and generally made by their own College: Yet the Choice was twice put into the Power of the People by their Tribunes; but was soon after the first time restored to the College by Sulla, and the 2d time Cæsar,

having gain'd the absolute Power, took it from the People; and making himself Pontifex Maximus, all his Successors in the Empire constantly bore the Title, even after they became Christians, till Gratian, about the Year of Christ 380, rejected it.

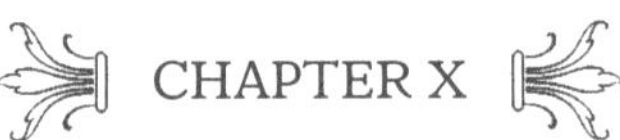

## CHAPTER X

55 Agamemnon, King of Mycenæ in Peloponesus, and Brother of Menelaus, was General of all the Forces of the Greeks, that went against Troy. He makes this Wish, in Homer's Iliad B. or Book 2. v. 372 in the Greek; in English thus, by A. Pope, V. 440.

*To him the King, How much thy Years excel*
*In Arts of Council, and of speaking well:*
*Oh would the Gods, in Love to* Greece, *decree*
*But ten such Sages as they grant in thee,*
*Such Wisdom soon should* Priam*'s Force destroy,*
*And soon should fall the haughty Towers of Troy.*

56 Both Plutarch, in the Life of Cato, and C. Nepos say, he went into the Service at the Age of 17; and we saw before at Note 13, that he was in it at the Retaking of Capua in his 20th Year. He went Quæstor in his 30th Year, with Scipio Africanus, into Sicily and Afric, where (his Office engaging him in the Business of the publick Accounts, and Scipio being of a free Temper and a generous Disposition) they wisely disagreed; in so much that Cato, repairing to Rome, and there applying himself to Q. Fabius Maximus, whom he principally chose [as we saw before at Note 11] for his Patron, this Affair, together with a Complaint of the Locrians, a People situate near Sicily, was laid before the Senate; and being highly exaggerated by Fabius, a Prætor and two Tribunes were appointed, and very close Orders given them to inquire into Scipio's Conduct: Who returning, confirmed the Complaint of the Locrians; but in relation to Scipio, as Plutarch gives it, in the Life of Cato, they reported, that when not otherwise engaged, he took his Diversion and enjoy'd himself with his Friends; but at the same time he neglected no Business. Livy, on the other hand, who is much larger in his Account of the Whole [Bo. 29. c. 22.] without mentioning Cato at all, but making Fabius the chief Complainant, represents

those Ambassadors charmed with the excellent Order they found both the Fleet and Army in, of which they made Report to the Advantage of Scipio in the highest Degree.



Scipio embark'd for Afric in the 550th Year of Rome, when Cato must have been about 30 Years old. He was Consul in the 559th, and had Spain for his Province, where he obtain'd signal Victories over the Spanish Inhabitants, (for the Carthaginians, in the late Peace made 6 Years before, had intirely surrendred to Rome, and quitted all their Pretences to Spain) and the next Year, on his Return to Rome, viz. 560, he led a Triumph for these Victories. Three Years after this he went *Tribunus militum*, or Tribune of the Soldiers [generally of the Infantry, a kind of Major General of the Foot] under Manius Acilius Glabrio, one of the Consuls, in the 563d of Rome, into Macedon and Thessaly, to oppose Antiochus Magnus, King of Syria; who, under Pretence of asserting the Liberties of Greece (for which there was no Occasion, since T. Q. Flaminius, as in Note 3. had put the Greeks in Possession of these five Years before) made War against the Romans; and posting himself in the famous Straits of Thermopylæ (where Leonidas, and 300 Lacedemonians, opposing Xerxes so gallantly, died) was by Cato's Conduct, in surmounting the Clifts, intirely defeated. He was chosen Censor 11 Years after his Consulship, in his 50th Year; on which Livy, Bo. 39. as quoted before at Note 7. is large.

As to his Age, as he was born [as in Note 12] in the 520th Year of Rome; and Cicero in his *Brutus* gives the Consuls of the Year he died in, who by the Fasti were so in the 605th Year; he should have died, according to that Account, in his 85th Year: But this directly contradicts the Historian Livy, whose Business it was more exactly to consult and consider the Annals, and who [at Note 7] positively says, he impleaded S. Galba in his 90th Year; and C. Nepos, another good Historian, says, he was engaged in publick Affairs 80 Years; by which he should have lived to near 100 Years. These Historians therefore, are most to be depended on: For Cicero has been observed in some other Cases to miss in his Computations.

The *Rostra* was a publick Place in Rome, where the Orators, and those who spoke to the People on any publick Affair, whether in relation to the Laws or Judgments, &c. delivered what they had to say. This Name Rostra, was given it, from its being built up with the Beaks of the Ships, that the Romans, on taking

Antium, a Sea-port Town to the South-east of the Mouth of Tiber, and destroying their Fleet, brought as Trophies to Rome. *Vid. Liv. l.* 8. *c.* 14. *in fine.* And not as Lipsius says, (*de Magnitud. U. Romæ, lib.* 3. *c.* 8.) from those gained at the Battle of Antium, fought by Augustus some Years after this Discourse was wrote.

57 This was some Officer then noted for his great Strength, not elsewhere mention'd, that I know of.

58 Massinissa, Son of Gala, King of the Massylians, a Nation of the Numidians in Africa. His Story is extreamly remarkable. The two Scipio's in Spain, mentioned before at Note 50, but largely spoke of in Note 97. sent Legates to Syphax, King of the Numidians, to engage his Friendship to the Romans; in which they succeeded. The Carthaginians provok'd at this, prevailed with Gala to make War upon Syphax; which he accordingly did, by sending his Son Massinissa, a Youth of great Spirit, tho' but 17 Years of Age, with an Army against him. This young General intirely defeated Syphax; and being in the Interest of the Carthaginians, he went over as their Ally into Spain where he very much contributed to the Overthrow of the Scipio's. His Father Gala dying, his Brother Œsalce, Massinissa's Uncle, succeeded him; and on his Death soon after, Gala's Son Capusa, who, being young and weak, one Mezelulus of the royal Blood, rebelled against him, raised an Army, and fought the young King, who with most of his Army was cut off. Yet Mezetulus on his Removal claim'd not the Crown to himself, but set up Lacumaces, another younger Son of Gala, to whom he pretended to be Guardian. Massinissa (who objected not to his Uncle Œsalce's Succession to his Father, for so the Law of their Country appointed) hearing in Spain of his Uncle's and Cousin's Death, hastned over to Afric, landed in Mauritania, and obtained of its King Bocchar, 4000 Men, with whom he march'd into Massylia; and meeting there only 500 of his Countrymen, who went to receive him, he, according to Promise, dismissed his Escort, the Moors.

His Numbers increasing, and gaining one Battle, Lacumaces fled to Syphax. Massinissa, doubting his own Strength, proposed an Accommodation; of which Syphax approved at first, till Asdrubal of Carthage, shew'd him the Danger of such a Neighbour, and prevail'd with him

Notes for page 30

to carry on the War. This he accordingly did, and overthrew Massinissa, who with a few about him, fled to the Mountains, and there liv'd on Plunder. Syphax sent a Commander (whose Name also was Bocchar) with Forces against him, who intirely defeated and pursued him to a large rapid River: Massinissa, with four more, took it; two of whom were carried away by the Violence of the Stream, and perished; but Massinissa, tho' sorely wounded, with the other two escaped. Bocchar and his Men, believing them all lost, reported the Matter so to Syphax, to his and his People's no small Joy, as well as to that of Asdrubal. But Massinissa, as soon as he had recovered of his Wound, to their great Mortification, and to the equal Joy of his Friends, appeared again, as if he had dropt out of the Clouds, and in a little Time collecting an Army of 6000 Foot and 4000 Horse, was ready to oppose Syphax; who then began to consider Masinissa as an Enemy that would require his utmost Thought and Care. He therefore raised a large Army, march'd himself against him, and sending his Son Vermina with another Body round, to attack him on the Rear while he himself engaged in the Front, Masinissa was intirely routed again; and it was only by his singular Dexterity, that he narrowly escaped the great Diligence Vermina used in the Pursuit: But from that Time he was obliged to keep private and at a Distance, till the Romans landed.

In this Time Asdrubal, apprehending the Romans might as formerly make a Descent on Afric, judged it necessary to bring Syphax into a strict Alliance with Carthage: For which end he gave him his Daughter Sophonisba, a fine Woman, in Marriage. Scipio landing, sent Lælius into the Country before him. Masinissa then presently appeared; and joining him, drew great Numbers of Numidians to their Assistance. Their first Battle was with Syphax, whom they defeated, and took himself, with his beautiful Queen Sophonisba, Prisoners. She fell at Masinissa's Feet, imploring his Mercy, as of the same Country with her, and that she might rather die, than be delivered up to the Pride of the Romans. This he not only promised; but, charmed with her Looks and Behaviour, married her himself the same Day. Scipio highly offended at this, reproved him for it; and he knowing his Dependance must be wholly on the Romans, to be as just to his Bride as lay in his Power, and to keep his Word to her, sent her a Bowl of Poison with a proper Message, which she bravely took, and, as she desired, died free. This is all related by Livy, *lib.* 29. Massinissa, by the Favour of the Romans, greatly enlarged his Dominions. He reigned 60 Years; was always faithful to the Romans, and left this younger Scipio his Executor. *Liv. lib. 50. Epit.*

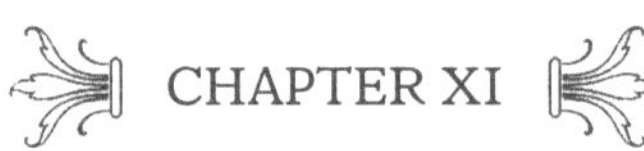

## CHAPTER XI

59 Cato's *Origines* was a Work much esteemed by the Romans, but is lost to us. C. Nepos informs us, that its first Book contained the Actions of the People of Rome, (probably to the Time of the first Punic or Carthaginian War) the 2d and 3d gave the Origin or first Rise of all the Cities of Italy; the 4th was the History of the first Punic War; the 5th gave the second, which was in his own Time; in the following he related their other Wars, till the Conquest of Lusitania, now Portugal; which I judge to have been the Conquest mention'd by Livy, *lib.* 41. *c.* 11. for which L. Posthumius triumphed about 20 Years before this Discourse; for I find Sergius Galba, whom Nepos names, no-where mention'd in relation to these Wars.

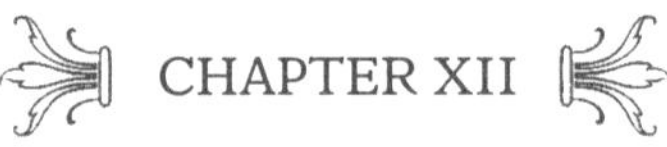

## CHAPTER XII

60 Archytas, of Tarentum, was of Pythagoras's School, contemporary with Plato, whose Life he saved when Dionysius, the Tyrant of Syracuse, intended, for some free Discourse, to put him to Death. He governed the Tarentines, and seven times commanded their and their Confederates Armies. He was a great Mathematician and Mechanic, and made a Wooden Pigeon that would by Springs fly about in the Air. A. Gellius, *lib.* 10. 12. Diog. Lærtius, Strabo, Suidas, Ælian, Athenæus, speak of him. Horace remembers him also, in that Ode, beginning with,

> *Te maris et terræ numeroque carentis arenæ*
> *Mensorem cohibent Archyta*—— *Lib.* 1. *Od.* 28.

61 This was in the Year of Rome 433. The Story is so remarkable, and may be so usefully applied, that it is well worth knowing. The Samnites were the toughest Enemies the Romans had to deal with in Italy. They had been at War with them at times for 30 Years; and now resolving, if possible, intirely to

Notes for page 36

subdue them, the two Consuls here named, led the better Part of the Forces of Rome against them. Pontius used Means to deceive and decoy them, till they unwarily marched into a Vale, surrounded on all Sides, but at two Defiles, with thick unpassable Forests and Mountains, and coming to the Out-let, they found it closed up with vast Trees and Stones heaped together by the Samnite Army, who, much contrary to the false Informations, artfully given the Roman Consuls by suborned Shepherds, were there watching their Enemy; and when they would have return'd by the Way they came in, they found that Entrance in the same Condition with the other. The Romans thus shut up, and in a manner besieged could find no possible Means of extricating themselves, or to prevent their starving.

The Samnite General Pontius having them at this Disadvantage, sent to his Father Herennius Pontius, who was in great Repute for his Virtue and Wisdom, for his Advice what he should do with the Enemy then in his Power. The Father advised his Son to dismiss them honourably, and make a Peace with Rome; for this generous Action would for ever engage the Friendship of the Romans. The Son could not think of intirely giving up such an Advantage, and therefore sent to his Father again, desiring him to consider further of it. He then advised the General to put them all to the Sword; for by this, Rome would for a long Time be so weakned, that their Neighbours might for that Time at least live in Peace. This last Advice the Son thought too cruel, and, by the Advice of the Army, sending for his Father, prayed his Presence; who being very old, to oblige his Son, came to the Camp in a Waggon, and there supported both Parts of his Advice with Reasons, said he knew no Medium, and returned. But the Son, resolving to take a middle Course, gave all the Romans their Lives; concluded Articles of Peace, to be confirmed by the Senate; took Hostages; but disarmed them all, and obliged the whole Army, with the Consuls, to pass or creep *sub hastam*, under the Pike; a Mark of the greatest Ignominy. And thus they all returned home disarmed, in the utmost Confusion; which was also greater in the City, than if they had been utterly defeated or destroyed.

Posthumius the Consul hereupon told the Senate, they were not obliged by what he and his Collegue Veturius had done; advised that they who signed the Articles, might be sent back bound to the Samnites, with the Officer called a *Fecial*, a kind of Herald, to deliver them. This being done, and these Men

Notes for page 36

delivered to Pontius bound, Posthumius said, he was now no longer a Roman, but a Samnite; and having his Feet at Liberty, kick'd the Fecial Officer, and said, Now Rome has just Cause to make War on the Samnites, since one of those People (meaning himself) had violated the Law of Nations, and abused a sacred Officer of the Romans. Pontius justly provoked at this Fraud and Prevarication of the Romans, in a most reasonable Speech [as Livy, the Roman Historian, himself gives it, *lib.* 9. *c.* 11.] refusing to receive the Consuls, highly upbraided the Romans for their Breach of Faith, loudly expostulated with those present, and insisted, That if they had any Regard to Justice, Honour, or for the Gods they swore by, they should either ratify the Peace made on his giving the Army their Lives and Freedom, or they ought to return to the same Place they had been by his Favour delivered from, where their Arms should be all restored to them, to use again as they pleased. And then he ordered those who were bound to be untied, and, telling them he had nothing to say to them, the Samnites would now insist on the Articles, which was all they had in Exchange for the whole Army of Rome; bid them go about their Business. Accordingly they went home.

The Romans immediately carried on the War against them, in which Pontius had many Engagements with them; but at length, upon an intire Defeat of his Army, by Fabius Gurges, whom he had vanquished but a little before, he was taken Prisoner by him, led in Triumph at Rome 25 Years after the other Action, and ungenerously there put to Death.

There is another Case in the Roman History, exactly parallel to this; when Mancinus the Consul, being with his Army caught by the Numantines in Spain, much in the same Manner, for making a Peace that displeased the Senate, was sent back, and in the same Manner delivered to that People, but refused by them; and then by a fresh Army, under the Command of this great Man, but ill employed, Scipio Æmilianus, they were famished to Death, and utterly destroyed; on no other Pretence, than to cover the Scandal the Romans conceived they underwent in being so shamefully beaten.

62 There is no such Pair of Consuls together to be found in the Roman Fasti. In the various Readings of the Text, there is, instead of L. Æmilius and Appius Claudius, Lucius Camillus and Publius Claudius; who truly were Consuls in

the 400th Year of Rome: And this well suits Plato's Age; for he must then have been about 42 Years.

63 This is touched in Note 3, but it requires to be further spoke to. Val. Maximus, *l.* 2. *c.* 9. gives the Story, much as Cicero has it here; but Livy, the chief of the Roman Historians, delivers it otherwise. He says, *Lib.* 39. *c.* 42. That Lucius Q. Flaminius, going with the Army into Gaul, prevailed with a noted beautiful Youth (whom he calls Philip of Carthage) on great Promises made to him, to go with him to the Camp: That the Lad, in toying with the Consul, often used to upbraid him, that, to gratify him, he had lost the Pleasure of the Shows of Gladiators [or Fencers] that were then exhibiting in Rome: That as they were one Evening at Supper, and merry over their Liquor, Word was brought to the Consul, That a noble Boian [these were a People of Gaul] was come over with his Children to submit himself, and crave the Protection of the Romans: That desiring to see the Consul himself, the Gentleman was called in; and while he was addressing himself to him by an Interpreter, Lucius asked his —— He-Miss, whether (since he complained of losing the Sight of Gladiators dying at Rome) he would be pleased to see that Gaul die there before him? That, the Lad jestingly consenting, Lucius taking his Sword that hung by him, rose up and gave the Man, as he was speaking, a Wound in the Head, and then, as he endeavoured to escape, pursued and run him through the Body.

Livy gives this from Cato's own Speech, which he seems to have then had by him; and blames another Historian, for delivering it wrong, and only upon Hear-say, as by this of Livy, Cicero seems to have done here. Plutarch tells it both Ways, in the Lives both of T. Flaminius and of Cato.

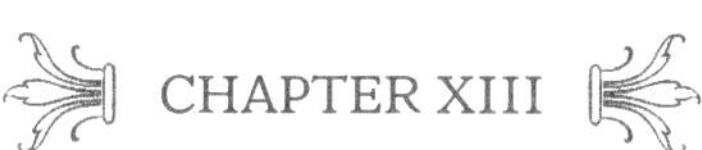

## CHAPTER XIII

64 This Cineas, in studying Eloquence, was a Hearer of the famous Orator Demosthenes of Athens, and was thought to express his Manner the nearest of any of his Age. He afterwards attended Pyrrhus, who said of him, that he had gained more Places by Cineas's Eloquence, than by his own Arms. Plutarch gives this fine Relation of him, That seeing Pyrrhus bent on his Expedition into Italy, [see Notes 25, 26.] taking a proper Opportunity for it; These Romans, says

# Notes for Chapter XIII

Notes for page 38

Cineas to Pyrrhus, are accounted a very brave People, and are said to have subdued many valiant Nations about them; should it please God to grant us to conquer them pray what are we to do next? Why then, said Pyrrhus, all the rest of Italy will lie open to us: For when once we have subdued Rome, no other Nation there will pretend to resist us; and Italy, you know, as it is a rich and large Country, will be a noble Aquisition. That it would, said Cineas; and pray, what are we to do next? Then answered Pyrrus, As Sicily lies close by it, and now since Agathocles's Death, is all in Confusion, we will step over thither, and make that easily our own also. And shall we rest there? said Cineas. No, answered Pyrrhus; Carthage and Africa lie so near, and so tempting, that we must have these also; nor will it be difficult, since Agathocles himself was once so near taking Carthage, and with no very great Force neither. And what Course are we to take next? said Cineas. Then you very well know, replied Pyrrhus, that those who have hitherto given us so much Trouble, will no longer be able to oppose us: We shall get the better of all our Adversaries. That's very probable, said Cineas, when you have made so many large Conquests, you may easily get Macedon, and reduce all Greece to Reason: But after all these mighty Atchievements, pray Sir, be pleased to tell me what Use we are to make of them and what is to follow next? Why then truly, Cineas, said Pyrrhus, smiling, we'll sit down, be merry and drink, and enjoy ourselves in Quiet with our Friends. And if that be all, answered Cineas, pray, what hinders us from doing just the same, as Things now stand? You well know, you have now, as much as You then would, all the necessary Means for this, in your Power; and you may be as merry, as quiet, and enjoy your Friends as much as you will ever be able to do, after all the vast Fatigues and Hazards, and Effusion of Blood, these Undertakings must necessarily be attended with; and after you have not only involved infinite Numbers of People, who have never offended you, in all the dire Calamities of War, but must also expose your best Friends to numberless Dangers.

Pyrrhus was not well pleased with this Close. He proceeded, as has been noted, to Italy; and being there disappointed, he passed over into Sicily, where he was more so; and returning to Italy, he was there soundly beat by the Romans, and obliged to fly. At home in Epirus and Greece he continued restless; and at length, in Argos, had his Brains beat out, by a Potsheard thrown from the Top of a House by an old Woman. His Life is in Plutarch, which see.

# Notes for Chapter XIII

Notes for page 38

65 See Note 26.

66 See Note 27, and for Fabricius, Note 25.

67 Epicurus is meant here, who was then living: For Lærtius says, he was born the 3d of the 109th Olympiad, seven Years after Plato's Death, and died in the 2d of the 127th Olympiad, in the 72d Year of his Age: He therefore must have lived nine Years after Pyrrhus's Expedition into Italy. Epicurus had in his own Time a very ill Character given him by the Philosophers of other Sects, and the same has thro' all succeeding Ages stuck to him; but many think him much wronged. His Physics, or Opinions of Nature, were grossly absurd in many Things; but his Morals, that are so much decried, were very different from what they are generally accounted. He proposed Pleasure, 'tis true, for the End of Action; but that Pleasure was to consist in the Tranquility of the Mind, and inward Satisfaction, and not in voluptuous Enjoyments: For he is said to have been perfectly temperate himself, and that all his Doctrine tended to the same. He wrote much, but nothing of his remains, save what Lærtius has in his tenth Book, which is wholly bestowed on his Life and Doctrine. Gassendus explained it in some large Volumes.

68 Publius Decius Mus, was the first time Consul in the 442d Year of Rome; and this 4th time, when he fell, was in the 459th. The two Consuls Quintus Fabius Maximus [there were divers from time to time of that Name of the same Family] being, the 5th time Consul, and this Decius (as has been noted) the 4th, were engaged in a doubtful and almost desperate Battle with the Gauls and Samnites; with whom two other Nations, the Etrurians (or Tuscans) and the Umbrians, were also at the same time Confederates against Rome. When the Fight had continued long, nearly equal on both Sides, and at length the Gauls made some Impression on the left Wing where Decius commanded, and his Men began to break and fly, nor could he by any Means restrain them; invoking his Father's Name, who had before devoted himself, he called to him the Pontiff that attended, to repeat to him the Form to be used in Devoting; which he took in the same Manner his Father had done, and in the same Manner also the Romans got the Day: For the flying Forces, hearing what their General had

Notes for page 38

done, rallied of themselves, and with new Spirits vigorously attacked their Enemies, and bore all before them.

To devote one, is to offer him up as accursed for an atoning Sacrifice, for the Safety of others: And the Method of it is curious enough to render it worth knowing. We have it particularly in Livy, in his Account of this Decius his Father Devoting himself, [*Lib.* 8. *c.* 9.] in the 414th Year of Rome; and it was thus: The Romans and the Latins after a long Alliance differing, they drew out equal Forces and engaged. Victory inclining to neither Side, and one of the Consuls, Decius, almost despairing of it, resolved on a desperate Action, which he hoped might secure it. He called on the Pontiff who was with him, to repeat before him the solemn Form of Devoting; for he would offer himself up, he said, for an Atonement for the Army. The Pontiff ordered him to put on the Civic Gown; and covering his Head, to put up his Hand within his Gown under his Chin, and treading on a Weapon, to repeat these Words after him:

> *O Janus, Jupiter, Father Mars, Quirinus, Bellona! Ye Home Gods, Foreign Gods, Indigetes and lower Gods, who have us and our Enemies in your Power! and ye Infernal Gods! I pray, adore and beseech you, that you will make good and prosper Strength and Victory to the Roman People; and that you will confound, terrify and do to Death the Enemies of the Romans! As I have now conceived in Words, so, for the Public Weal, Army, Legions and Auxiliaries of the Roman People, I devote* [or accurse] *the Legions and Auxiliaries of their Enemies, together with my Self, to the Infernal Gods, and to the Earth.*

This done, he sent Notice of it to the other Consul T. Manlius. Then putting on his Armour and mounting his Horse, he rode into the thickest of the Enemy, and carried Destruction before him, till he was cut in Pieces: Which was one necessary Part of the Ceremony; for without it, all the rest would have been void. And therfore, when this Man's Grandson Publius Decius, being Consul with Sulpicius, in the 2d Battle the Romans had with Pyrrhus; and it was reported, that he, after his Grandfather's and Father's Example, would also devote himself; Pyrrhus apprehensive lest it might give some Terror to his Men, sent Word to the Consul, that he should leave off Fooling; for that he would take Order, if he attempted it, to disappoint him, he should not fall in that

Manner in the Field, but meet with a Death less to his liking. He neither did, however, nor had proposed to attempt it. Livy, *lib.* 8. and Plutarch in Pyrrhus.



69 The Romans having had great Success for four Years against the Carthaginians, in their first War with them, by Land; but lying exposed to them by Sea, as having no Fleet, resolved to build one; and ordered the Consuls, of whom this Duillius was one, to proceed to the Work; and in sixty Days (Livy says) after the Timber was fall'n, they had [*incredible*] 160 Ships of War compleated, and at Anchor: To furnish which with Men, those designed for the Service, were taught all the Motions and Management of Oars, in which, while their Ships were building, they were exercised on shoar. But finding on Trial these Ships much more unwieldy than those of their Enemies; to ballance this, they contrived an Engine placed at their Heads, by which, when closed in with another Ship, they would grapple and hold her so fast, that she could not possibly get clear. They framed also on the Engine a kind of Platform to stand on, and enter other Ships by it. Thus they fought at Sea, as if they had been on Land, Hand to Hand with their Enemies: And in the first Engagement, Duillius sunk 14 Ships, killing 3000 Men, and took 31 Ships more with 7000 Prisoners; for which he triumphed.

70 Commonly called *Idæmater*, the Idæan Mother. In the 549th Year of Rome, a little before Annibal left Italy, the Roman Armies were seized with so violent a Sickness, that they were in Danger of being all lost; nor were the Carthaginians clear from it: And about the same Time dreadful Prodigies from the Heavens were seen, as Raining Stones, (of which we hear so often in their History, that we may reasonably believe they must have meant nothing but large Hail by it; for they accounted even great Thunder-Storms a Denunciation of the Anger of their Gods.) Those who had the *Sibylls* Books in keeping, consulting them on these Calamities, said, they found an Oracle there, declaring, that when a foreign Enemy should invade Italy, the Country might be delivered from them, if the Idæan Mother were brought from Pessinus to Rome. This was a Place in Phrygia in Asia Minor. And for this the Romans fitted out five large Ships, with a solemn Embassy to Attalus, the King of those Parts, to request the Favour.

# *Notes for Chapter XIV*

Notes for pages 42-43

They took the Oracle of Delphi in their Way, to consult that also, and know their Success: The Answer was favourable, further telling them, "The worthiest Man of Rome must be appointed to receive the Goddess into the City." Attalus, to oblige the Romans, tho' they had then no Intercourse with Asia, granted their Request; and shewed them a great Stone, which the Inhabitants called by that Name: And they brought her Divinity to the River Tiber, where Scipio Nassica was appointed, as the best Man in Rome, to receive her. Thus Livy, Bo. 29. c. 10, &c. Herodian, who wrote the History of the Reigns of ten Emperors, about the Year of Christ 240, in the Life of Commodus, tells a long Story of that Goddess, and the Devotion yearly paid her at Rome: He says, The Image was framed by no mortal Hands, but sent down from Heaven by Jupiter; that the Ship that brought her, sticking fast in the River Tiber, a Vestal Virgin, who was accused of Unchastity, to prove her Innocence, hawled the Ship along, only by her Girdle. But Livy, writing the History of the Time, says nothing of this: For Miracles are often best known some Centuries after they are said to have been wrought.

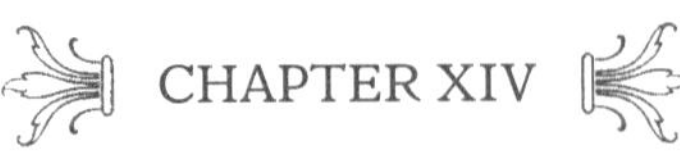

## CHAPTER XIV

71 In Xenophon's Works there is a Tract called the *Symposion,* or Feast, consisting of the pleasant Discourses of the Guests; which is more natural than that of Plato's.

'Tis said of Old Cato, that he could be free enough sometimes with the Creature: Hence Horace, *l.* 3. *Ode* 21.

*Narratur et prisci Catonis*
*Sæpe mero caluisse virtus.*
Old Cato would, 'tis said, with Wine
Make his reverend Face to shine.

72 Turpio Ambivius was a famous Actor in Rome, about the 590th Year of the City. He is mentioned in what is called the *Didascalia,* of 4 of the 6 Comedies we have of Terence, to have been the principal Actor of them.

73 Caius Sulpicius Gallus, the first of the Romans [Pliny says, *lib.* 2. *c.* 12.] who applied himself to the Study of the Stars, in which he was very famous.

# *Notes for Chapter XIV*

Notes for page 44

Being Tribunus Militum in the Army commanded by Paulus Æmilius, the Day before the great Battle, in which Perseus, King of Macedon, was defeated, and his Kingdom thereupon made a Province, [see Note 24] he gave publick Notice to the Army, that the ensuing Evening the Moon would be eclipsed and darkned from the 2d to the 4th Hour, [that was then, from near 10 to near 12 at Night in our Account] and as this could be foretold, by the Knowledge only of the Course and Motions of the Sun and Moon, they should not therefore be surprized at it, or account it a Prodigy. But the Macedonians, it seems, were not so happy, as to have such a skilful Adviser amongst them; for the Eclipse happened accordingly, and the Greeks were much terrified.

Livy, who [*lib.* 44. *c.* 37.] relates this, says, it was the Night before the 4th of September, which both Calvisius and Petavius having calculated, find to have fallen on the 21st of June, 168 Years before Christ, according to our present Account; for the Roman Calendar was at that Time, for the Reasons given by Censorinus [*cap.* 20.] exceedingly perplexed and uncertain, till Julius Cæsar in his 3d Consulate, being then also Pontifex Maximus, 45 Years before Christ, regulated it, and established our present Julian Account. This Sulpicius Gallus, two Years after that Battle, was Consul himself; and Paulus Æmilius, the Consul and General in it, natural Father to this Scipio [see Note 24] was his great Friend.

74 Cneius Nævius, see Note 30.

75 Marcus Accius Plautus: We have 20 of his Comedies still extant, and amongst them, those two here named.

Livius Andronicus was the first Roman Poet, mentioned by their Writers: There is nothing of his remaining, but a few short Fragments from the Quotations of Grammarians; according to Cicero in *Tusc. Quæst. lib.* 1. as also in his Brutus. He acted that first Piece in the 512th Year of Rome, 240 Years before Christ.

76 The same with Publius Crassus mention'd before. See Note 49.

77 Marcus Cethegus is mention'd by Cicero in his Brutus, or Book *de claris Oratoribus*, as the first Orator amongst the Romans worth Notice, or that bore

that Character: And his Name was the more famous for the honourable Mention Ennius made of him in his Annals, some of whose Verses Cicero there quotes, and says, he was Consul 9 Years before Cato, that is, in the 550th Year of Rome, 204 Years before Christ, the 15th of the second Punic War.

## CHAPTER XV

78 This Book of Cato's, *de Re Rustica,* is still extant, and is the oldest Book in Prose, that we have in the Latin Tongue; but does no great Honour to the Author.

79 We have one, or as some account them, two short Books of Hesiod's, called *Works and Days,* with two others, in which, among some other Things, he lays down several Rules for Husbandry: And from these Virgil copies in his *Georgics,* but very much enlarged and far exceeded him.

80 This seems to be a Lapse of Memory in Cicero; for there is no such Passage in Homer, as we now have his Works, as that Lærtes was dunging his Fields. If any where, it should be in the 24th or last Book of the *Odyssey.* But there Spondanus, on the 226th Verse, Listraonta phyton, &c. notes, that Gifanius had observed this Passage here in Cato, to be a Mistake in Cicero. Yet Cicero in his Time might perhaps have read it in that Sense in Homer, as *koprizonta,* or *kopreuonta,* Dunging, instead of *listraonta* or *listreuonta,* Levelling the Plants; which is indeed an odd Expression.

## CHAPTER XVI

81 Manius Curius Dentatus, for his History see Note 26 before. —— I shall only add here, That Plutarch [*Apophth. Rom.*] says, he was then boiling (others say roasting) Turneps for his Supper: And Val. Maximus, who has the same Story [*lib.* 4. *c.* 3] says, he was eating out of a Wooden Dish, and that by his Furniture we may judge what were his Viands, &c.

82 Lucius Quinctius Cincinnatus was Consul of Rome in the 293d Year of it, 459 Years before Christ; being surrogated in the Place of Valerius Poplicola, who was kill'd in recovering the Capitol from Herdonius [*Liv. l.* 3. *c.* 19.] the

# Notes for Chapter XVII

Notes for page 55

Roman's being exceedingly pressed by the Volsci 2 Years after, and finding themselves obliged to appoint a Dictator, they chose Quinctius, who then lived on his small Farm, that had consisted at first but of seven Roman Jugera, which makes in the Whole but about four and a half English Acres; but by paying a Fine for his Son Sæso, was reduced to four Jugera, or two and a half Acres only. On this Farm the Messenger sent to him from the Senate, found him at Work; who desiring him to put on his Gown, that he might receive the Pleasure of the Senate, he left his Plow, and called on his Wife Racilia (for her Name is also remembred) to bring it to him; he put it on, and was then saluted by him, Dictator; an Office so high, that it superseded all the other Powers, as has been noted before.

Livy, *lib.* 3. *c.* 26. pursues the Story, the Sum of which was this: He repaired to Rome, raised Levies, marched against the Enemy, who then besieged the Consul with his Army in the Camp, subdued, and made them all pass *sub jugo,* a Mark of Subjection; triumphed for his Victory; and, having settled Affairs, laid down that great Office, which of Right he might have held for 6 Months, the 16th Day after he entred on it. But the other Part of the Story, of his causing Mælius to be put to Death, was 20 Years after, when in a great Old Age he was chose Dictator again, on purpose to quell that Conspiracy. Livy, Bo. 4. c. 13, &c. has the Story. Both Livy and Val. Maximus, *l.* 4. *c.* 4. have some fine Reflections on the first Part of this Account of Cincinnatus.

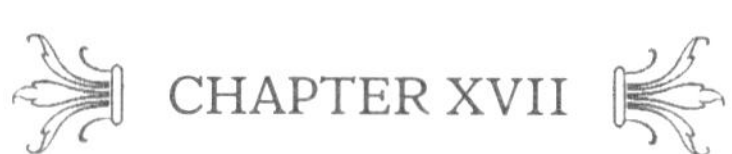

## CHAPTER XVII

83 Marcus Valerius Corvus or Corvinus. Livy, an Historian of great Gravity, Bo. 7. c. 26. tells this very odd Story of him: That being a Tribune of War, when the Roman Army under the Consul L. Furius Camillus, was to engage that of the Gauls, a Champion of that nation, remarkable both for his Size and Armour, stepping out, challenged the whole Roman Army, to send out any one of their bravest Men to fight him in single Combat. This Valerius took the Challenge, met him, and had no sooner began to engage, than a Crow or Raven [but *Corvus* is properly a Raven, tho' often rendred a Crow] lighted on his Helmet or Head-piece, and as often as he attack'd the Gaul, the Bird with his Bill and Claws did the same, flying at his Eyes and Face; which so confounded the Man, that he soon fell at Valerius's Feet, and was dispatch'd by him; and

then it flew away to the Eastward. Hence the Victor took the Name of Corvus or Corvinus, for it frequently occurs wrote both these Ways.

Val. Maximus, B. 8. c. 13. brings him as an Example of one that lived to a great and happy Old-Age, and says, he lived to 100 Years in Vigour both of Body and Mind; was six times Consul in the space of 47 Years; discharged the greatest Trusts; kept his Farm in most exquisite Order, and set a noble Example both in public and private Life. Pliny, *N. Hist.* B. 7. 48. mentions also his living to 100 Years, and that he was 6 times Consul, a Number that none besides, except C. Marius, before the Time of the Emperors ever equalled.

84 It may appear strange, that in this Discourse, where so many Instances are given of Persons who had attained to a great Age, and preserved in it their Vigour both of Body and Mind, Cato should be made to place the Commencement of Old-Age at the 46th Year of Life: But the Author Cicero had good Authority for it.

His Friend Varro, who always had the Character of the most learned of all the Romans, (as Censorinus, *de die natali, c.* 14. quotes him) divided the Life of Man into 5 Stages, each consisting of 15 Years: Those in the first Stage, he calls *Pueri,* Boys; in the 2d to 30 Years, *Adolescentes,* or Youths; in the 3d to 45, *Juvenes,* Young-Men, so called, he says, *a juvando,* from helping, because they asssisted the State in bearing Arms; from thence to 60 he calls *Seniores,* because on entring on that Stage, they begin *senescere,* to wax old; and from 60 to the End of Life, for which he fixes no Term, they are *Senes,* or Old-Men. Censorinus goes on to say, That Hippocrates the Physician divided Life into 7 Stages; the Terms of which are to 7, 14, 28, 35, 47, 56, and from thence to the End: That Solon made 10, each of 7 Years; to which Staseas added 2 more, making the last Term 84, or 12 times 7; which agrees with our present Tables, calculated by Dr. Halley, for valuing Annuities or Estates for Lives; for these make 85 the last Period, beyond which no Chance for living is estimated.

85 See Note 53 before.

86 Atilius Calatinus was Consul in the 496th Year of Rome; a short Account of whose Life is given by Aurelius Victor, amongst his illustrious Men; but there

appears nothing very particular in it, worth noting here. And it is to be questioned, whether in all the Monuments we have left us of Antiquity, there can any thing be now produced that should intitle him to so high a Character: For in Freinsheimius's Supplements to Livy, *lib.* 17. 22. there is a very disadvantageous Story of him and his Army, who in the first Punic War besieged Matistratum (now Mistretta) in Sicily, which the Inhabitants, obliging the Carthaginian Garrison, who were possessed of it, to surrender, or suffer them at least to surrender to the Romans; these without Mercy, and without Distinction of Sex or Age, put the greater Part of those Inhabitants to the Sword, and sold the rest for Slaves. Florus, *l.* 2. *c.* 2. gives him the Title of Dictator, but his Story is obscure. It was to save this Army, that Calpurnius Flamma, with 300 more, sacrificed their own Lives, as in Note 100.

87 Æmilius Lepidus was the first time Consul in the 567th Year of Rome, 8 Years after Cato; he was the second time in the 579th Year. He was chosen one of the Pontiffs in the Year 556, and Pontifex Maximus about the Year 571, and continued so near 30 Years, till his Death, which was about the Year 602. See Note 47. 'Tis noted in the Argument of the 48th Book of Livy, (for that and all the rest from the 45th are lost, but the Arguments remain) that he was 6 times appointed by the Censor's Prince of the Senate, and that he ordered his Sons at his Death, that his Funeral should be without any Pomp or Charge.

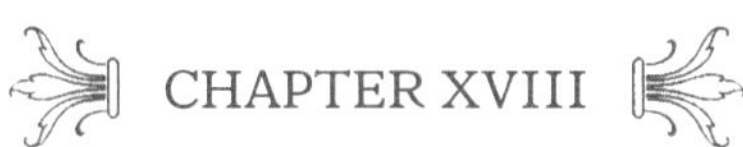

## CHAPTER XVIII

88 Mitio and Demea, Characters directly opposite in two Brothers; the latter of whom ruined his own Son by his Moroseness: The other by his mild Treatment of his Nephew, Brother to that Son, made him a fine Gentleman. Terence was contemporary with Cato, and his Comedy of the Adelphi was first acted in the Year of Rome 694, by the Names of the Consuls in the Didascalia prefixed to it.

## CHAPTER XIX

89 Cato's Son and Namesake died Prætor of the City of Rome, the same Year that Lepidus died, as in Note 87. viz. in the Year 602; and, as it is noted in the

same Argument of Livy there mention'd, viz. of Book 48. his Father gave him but a very mean Funeral, being able to afford no better, for that he was poor: [*M.P. Cato funus mortui filii, in Prætura, tenuissimo, ut valuit (nam pauper erat) sumptu facit.*] Which, considering the Offices that Cato bore, and his Frugality, adds not a little to his Character of Probity.

Plutarch gives this remarkable Story of Young Cato, in the Life of his Father, That being in the Army, under P. Æmilius, afterwards his Father-in-Law, in the great Battle fought with Perseus, King of Macedon, [Note 24] his Sword was struck out of his Hand, and he lost it; upon which, getting together a Company of Young Men of his Acquaintance, they made such an Impression on the Enemy, that they cleared the Way before them to the same Place again, where he recovered it amongst Heaps of the Slain: And adds, That in his Time [Plutarch's, above 250 Years after] Cato's Letter to his Son was extant, congratulating him on the Bravery of that Action.

90 See Note 24.—— These were Brothers to Scipio, but by half Blood, viz. the Sons of Paulus Æmilius by his 2d Wife, as Scipio was born of his first.

91 Tartessius, a City on the North Side of the River Bætis, now Guadalquivar, or the River of Sevil in Spain, and near the Mouth of it; supposed by some to be the Tarshish that Solomon sent his Ships to; the Phœnicians his Neighbours were the first ('tis said) who failed thither, where they found Silver in such Plenty, and got so much of it in Exchange for their Goods, that they could not carry it off, Aristotle says, but, to have the more of it, they threw away their Anchors, to make others of that Metal: But this is in his Book of wonderful Stories, and therefore may be more strange than true.

The Phoceans, a Greek Colony in Ionia, were the next who failed thither, in the Time of this Arganthonius, who was exceeding kind to them, inviting them to stay with him, and when they excused themselves, he gave them Money enough to wall in their Town against the Medes, who were then invading them. Herodotus gives the Story of Arganthonius and the Phoceans, l. 1. c. 163. The learned Bochart derives his Name from two Phoenician Words, *Arc-antho,* Long-lived. *Canaan, c.* 34.

# Notes for Chapter XX

## CHAPTER XX

Notes for page 65

92 Solon, see Note 45. It is there said, his Discourse with Cræsus, King of Lydia, is well known: But the Moral of it is so good and suitable to this Discourse, that it may properly come in here. Plutarch, in his Life of Solon, says, he was sent for by Cræsus; but Herodotus with more Probability, says, that absenting himself from Athens, after he had given them his Body of Laws, and traveling into Egypt, in his Return from thence thro' Asia Minor, he took Sardis, where Cræsus had his Royal Seat, in his Way. Cræsus was that Time accounted the richest King then known, and gloried much in his Magnificence, of which he was desirous Solon (whose Fame had reached those Parts) should be a Witness. Sending therefore for him to his Palace, and causing his Treasures and other Marks of his Grandeur to be shewn to him, when he afterwards came into his Presence, he asked Solon, who he thought was the happiest Man in the World? not doubting but he must answer, Cræsus himself. Solon said, the happiest Man he had known, was one Tellus.

Cræsus disappointed in his Answer, asked, what Prince or Hero was this Tellus? Solon replied, He was an honest Man of Athens, who lived above Want, and in good Repute brought up several Children as reputably; then being called to the Defence of his Country, signalized himself in the Battle with the Enemy, whom he overcame, and afterwards died fighting bravely in the same Cause; for which a Monument was erected in Honour of his Memory. Cræsus then asked Solon, whom he allowed to be happy in the next Degree? Solon said, next to Tellus he had known none happier than Cleobis and Biton, two Young Men of Argos, who, when their Mother wanted Creatures to draw her in her Carriage to the Temple of Juno, harnessing themselves, supplied their Place, and drew her 5 Miles to the Solemnity; where being arrived, and the whole Assembly greatly admiring and applauding their Dutifulness and Affection, their Mother fervently pray'd the Goddess, to reward her Sons filial Piety with the choicest Blessings she had in Store: And her Prayers were heard; for the Youths sleeping the same Night in the Temple, never awaked again, but crowning their Life with a glorious Action, by the special Favour of the Gods, honourably ended it.

Cræsus grew angry, and asked what he thought of Him? Solon in Answer made several fine Reflections on the Uncertainty of all Things in human Life; and concluded, That no Man was to be esteemed happy before his End was known. Upon which Cræsus dismissed him with Scorn. But afterwards had rueful Occasion to remember him. For, making War on Cyrus, King of Persia, he was defeated; then besieged in his Capital, taken Prisoner, and condemned to the Flames. When laid bound on the Pile, he cried out with a mighty Voice, *O Solon! Solon ! Solon!* Cyrus hearing him, stopt the Execution, to know the Meaning of it: Cræsus told the whole Passage; which so affected Cyrus, that he not only gave him his Life, but large Possessions with it, and took him into Favour. *Herodot. l.* 1. *Plut.* in Solon.

93 The Ancients called those *Tyrants,* who took the Government upon them against the People's Consent, without Regard to their Manner of Administring it.

Athens was a free State, under an Archon chosen by the People, and the Government popular. Pisistratus was a Citizen, wealthy, and for many excellent Qualities dear to the People; but secretly ambitious, which Solon discovered, tho' in vain: For tho' he was their Law-giver, the other was better heard, and at length gain'd his End by this Trick. There were at that Time two Factions in the State; the one of the Inland-Men, the other of the Shoar-Men and Citizens. Pisistratus being one Day in the Country, gave both himself and his Mules some Wounds, and driving into the City in that Condition in his Chariot, calling the People together, he bid them see how their Adversaries had used him, they had resolved to murther him, and he had narrowly escaped with his Life. The People hereupon, to secure him for the future, granted him a Guard of fifty Young Men. On the Foot of this Grant, he added what Number he thought fit; and then possessing himself of the Citadel, he ursurped the Government; yet made no Change either in the Magistracy or the Laws, save that he made himself Sovereign. But he was soon expell'd; recover'd it again by a stranger Contrivance, expell'd a 2d time, reinstated himself a 3d time, died possessed of it, and left it to his Children, who were expelled totally by Harmodius and Aristogiton, to whom Statues in Remembrance of this Action were erected.

94 Lucius Junius Brutus got his Name of brutus (*brute* or *stupid*) by his counterfeiting himself a Fool, or very silly, under the Reign of Tarquin the Proud, the last King of the Romans. He was Tarquin's own Sister's Son; but the

King, his Uncle, having amongst others put his elder Brother to Death, and becoming, by his Cruelty and Injustice, generally odious, Junius vow'd his Destruction; and the better to conceal it, affected that Appearance. He happen'd in riding from the Camp at Ardea towards Rome, to be in Company with his Kinsman Tarquinius Collatinus, Husband to Lucretia, whom the King's Son Sextus had ravished; when her Messenger meeting him, brought him the melancholy Account of it, Junius immediately laid hold on the Occasion, joined Collatinus the Husband, and Lucretius her Father, in their Revenge; and carrying the bloody Knife, with which Lucretia had stab'd herself, thro' the City, incited the People to rise, and assert their Liberty; which they effectually did, by expelling Tarquin and all his Race. Junius and Collatinus were hereupon chose the two first Consuls of Rome.

A Conspiracy to restore Tarquin was formed the same Year, in which Junius's own two Sons were engaged. These, with others, their Father caused to be lashed, and beheaded in publick in his Sight. Tarquin then, with the Veientes, his Allies, made War against Rome; and the two Armies meeting, Aruns the King's Son spying Junius at the Head of that of Rome, made directly up to him; and they so furiously engaged, that each run his Launce thro' the other's Shield and Body, and both died on the Spot. And the Roman Women mourned a whole Year for Brutus, as the Avenger of violated Chastity. *Liv. l. 1 & 2.*

95 See Note 68 at large.

96 Marcus Atilius Regulus, being in the Year 498 of Rome (256 Years before Christ) elected the second time Consul, in the Place of Q. Cædicius, who was chosen for that Year, but died soon after, embarking in the 9th Year of the Romans first War with the Carthaginians with his Collegue Lucius Manlius Vulso, in a Fleet of 330 Ships [tho' this was but the 5th Year since the Romans had any Fleet at all, see Note 69] and 140,000 Men, each Ship carrying about 420, engaged that of the Enemy, consisting of 360 Ships and 150,000 Men, commanded by Hanno and Hamilcar; sunk 30 of them, and took 63, with the Loss of 24 on their own Side, which were all sunk, and none taken. After this Victory they invaded Africa, and besieged and took Clupea. This Year being

Notes for page 67

expired, and new Consuls chosen, the Senate ordered Manlius to return with the Fleet and Army, excepting 40 Ships, 15,000 Foot, and 500 Horse, to be left under the Command of Regulus, during whose Government they continued to him as Pro-Consul. Regulus on receiving these Orders, remonstrated to the Senate, that if he continued longer absent from home, his Farm [which consisted only of 7 Jugera, or 4 and a half English Acres] would be ruined; for that his Hind or Manager that he had left on it, was dead, and another had run away with his Implements of Husbandry; and his Wife and Children would want Bread. Upon which the Senate appointed another to take Care of his Business and made good the Loss of what was stole from him, out of the publick Treasury. [*Val. max, l.* 4. *c.* 4.]

Regulus then augmenting his Troops, carried on the War successfully: But his Army lying near the River Bagrada, exceedingly suffered by a monstrous Serpent; which was Proof against all their Weapons, till they brought battering Engines against it. Silius Italicus says, it was 100 Yards in Length; but Pliny calls it only 120 Feet, or rather says, its Skin of that Length, was sent to Rome, together with its Jaw-Bone, which were kept there in a Temple, to the End of the Numantine War, that is, at least 120 Years. Valerius Maximus, l. 1. c. 8. from a Book of Livy (the 18th) now lost, is large in the Account of the Army's Sufferings by it, and says, it was more terrible and destructive, than all their Enemies Forces. Regulus having gained several Victories over the Carthaginians, was willing to make Peace with them, that he might himself have the Honour of ending the War; and the Carthaginians earnestly desired it, but the Terms he proposed appeared intolerable.

Xanthippus with some Mercenaries that they had sent for, arriving soon after from Lacedemon, observing their past Mistakes, at their Request took on him the Command of their Army, gave Regulus Battle, defeated him, and destroy'd his whole Army, then consisting (as Eutropius says) of 47,000 Men, excepting 2000 that escaped to Clupea; killing (as he gives it) 30,000, and taking 15,000 Prisoners, with Regulus himself, whom they sent in Chains to Carthage.

The Romans, notwithstanding this Loss, so vigorously carried on the War, that the Carthaginians five Years after sent Embassadors to Rome, and with them Regulus himself, to sue for Peace, or, if they could not obtain it, at least

for an Exchange of Prisoners; taking Regulus's Oath to return, if they did not succeed. [So sacred was an Oath by their Idols held by those Heathens, that are now so little regarded, even by Christian Princes, as well as others.] Coming to the Senate, Regulus behaved as a Carthaginian, whose Subject he said he was; but being required to give his Sentiments as a Roman, he advised both against a Peace and an Exchange. See Horace, Bo. 3. Ode 5. on this Subject.

His Friends on the Senate's taking his Advice, used their utmost Endeavours to disswade him from returning with the Embassadors, since he could expect nothing but the most cruel Treatment; nor would the Senate either encourage his Return or his Stay. But, his Oath and plighted Faith, he said, was of more Weight with him, than the Fear of Tortures or Death. He was unmoveably fixt, refused to see his Wife and Children, and embarked and returned in the same Company he came in.

Upon his Arrival, the Carthaginians incensed against him, caused him (as 'tis said) to be tormented to Death, by cutting off his Eye-lids, placing him erect on his Feet in a narrow Wooden Case drove full of sharp Spikes with their Points towards his Body; that he should not lean, or sleep, or rest, without running upon them; and exposing him in that Condition with his Face turned all Day to the Sun, till he expired. This Account of his Death, or the Substance of it, we have from Cicero in another Place, from Livy (*Argum.* 18. B.) Silius Italicus, Appian, Florus, Orofius, Zonaras, and others of the Ancients; and yet some late Critics reject it, and treat it only as a Fable. Palmerius (Jaques Paumier de Grantemesnil, a very learned Frenchman) in his Observations upon Appian, I think was the first who modestly proposed his Doubt, and gave his Reasons from Polybius's Silence in the Case, who, he says, has largely and prolixly given the History of the first Punic War; but chiefly from a Fragment of the 24th Book of Diod. Siculus, an excellent Historian, recovered, with others, last Century by Peiresc, and published by H. Valesius, in which there is this Expression in Greek, *'oti 'e meter*, &c. That the Mother —— of the Youths (that is Regulus's Wife and Mother of his Children) being deeply affected with her Husband's Death, and believing he died *(di' ameleian)* for want of Care being taken of him, caused [or advised] her Sons to treat the Prisoners (Bostar and Hamilcar that were delivered to them) with Rigour: Which they effectually did, by shutting them up together in a narrow Closet, without Victuals; so that

# *Notes for Chapter XX*

Notes for page 67

Bostar died in 5 Days, but Hamilcar continued till the Tribunes hearing of it, summoned the young Men, and threatning them with Death, for so highly dishonouring the State, obliged them to take due Care of them; upon which, throwing all the Blame on their Mother, they burnt Bostar's Body (according to the Roman Custom,) sent his Bones to Carthage to his Relations, and by proper Care restored Hamilcar to his Health and Strength. From which Passage in so faithful an Historian, Palmerius concludes, that the Family of the Atilij (i.e. of Regulus) to excuse that Barbarity, framed this Story of Regulus's Death, which, being to the Dishonour of the Nation they were at War with, and greatly hated, easily obtain'd Credit, and passed afterwards for Truth. Which indeed is not improbable. J. le Clerc, in a Note on Freinsheimius's Suppl. to Livy, (*lib. 18.*) joins in this with Palmerius.

But tho', for the sake chiefly of this late Discovery, I have already dwelt too long on it here; I cannot forbear adding, That Palmerius ought not to have said, that Polybius has given the History of this War largely or prolixly (*suse ne dicam prolixe,*) for he professes to give only a summary Account of it, as but preparatory to that of those Actions, with which he designed to begin his History: And therefore, tho' that War continued near 24 Years, and was, as he himself says, the greatest and most terrible that had ever been known, (the Romans, who had not one large Ship when it began, having lost 700 of five Banks of Oars, that is, of 300 Rowers each, and the Carthaginians 500 such, besides vast Numbers of others; and, as near as I can judge, not less than 300,000 Men on each Side;) yet Polybius bestows but about two Thirds of his first Book upon the Whole. Livy gave it 4 Books, from the 16th to the 19th inclusive; but these, with all the rest of his 2d Decad, from 11 to 20, are lost, and only the Arguments saved. Appian's History of it is also lost, and he only barely mentions it, with Regulus's Death, in his Beginning of that of their 3d War. Diodor. Siculus's Account of it is also lost; for of his 40 Books we have but 15, with that Fragment mention'd before, and some other few Scraps. Of Polybius's 40 Books there remain but 5 whole, with some Excerpts of 12 more, and some other Fragments. Of Livy's 140 Books there remain but 35, i.e. from 1 to 10, and from 21 to 45; but Freinsheimius has given us excellent Supplements of the rest. Of Appian's 24 Volumes of the Roman Wars there are about 8 or 9 left, for their Divisions are uncertain.

So that a great Part of the Roman History, and particularly of this great War, excepting what Polybius has given, as mention'd above, is to be pick'd out only from scattered Hints in other old Authors, or from Epitomes, as Florus, Eutropius, Justin, and such like: But there is nothing mention'd in any Part of these Notes, but what is taken from the Original Authors themselves. When or how Bostar and Hamilcar were taken, I find nothing, nor their Captivity mentioned, but in that Fragment of Diodore. They were committed to the Charge of Regulus's Family, as a Pledge for him, as he was a Captive at Carthage.

97 Cneius Cornelius Scipio and Publius Corn. Scipio, two Brothers, Sons of Cneius C. Scipio, in the Year of Rome 541, the 7th of the 2d Carthaginian War, and 212 before Christ, were at the Head of the Roman Forces in Spain, to defend their Dominions and Allies, and oppose the Carthaginians, who had three Armies there, commanded by Mago, Gisgo's Son, and Asdrubal; which last resolving to march with large Reinforcements, to join his Brother Annibal in Italy, by the same Route thro' Gaul, and over the Alpes that Annibal before had taken; the two Scipio's thought it incumbent on them, at any Hazard to prevent him; and they thought themselves strong enough to effect it, by the Help of the Auxiliaries they had raised: These were 30,000 Celtiberians, on whom they chiefly relied. But the Brothers dividing their Forces, and sending these Spaniards to march before them; Asdrubal falling in with their Leaders, found Means to perswade them to disband, and return home.

Thus denuded, they were exceedingly distressed, but by none more than by Masinissa, then a young Man, and in the Carthaginian Interest; who was afterwards so stanch a Friend to the Romans, and particularly to Scipio Africanus, Son to Publius, one of these Brothers. [See his Story in Note 58.] Publius entring on a desperate Action, he and his whole Army were cut off: And Cneius, before he knew any thing of his Brother's, had much the same Fate. Yet some of the Roman Forces escaped. Marcius, a single Roman Knight, of no Name or Character before, rallied these, and did such Wonders with them, that I know nothing in the Roman History, that exceeds his Actions and Conduct. Livy, B. 25.

98 Lucius Paulus Æmilius, Father to L. Paulus Æmilius at Note 24. He was Consul in the 537th Year of Rome, the 2d of the same War, with Caius Terentius

Notes for page 67

Varro, a Plebeian, raised to that Dignity by the Fury of the Commons and their Tribunes, who exclaimed against all the Patrician Order or Nobility, as if They were fond of continuing the War.

Paulus, a Man of excellent Conduct and great Experience, finding how unequally he was mated, did all he could to temper and moderate his Collegue's Rashness; but in vain. Annibal well knowing Varro's Character, and as well how to manage him, for some time play'd him to raise his Impatience, and then gave him Battle, near the Village Cannæ in Apulia; in which, Polybius says, 70,000 of the Roman Army fell, with both the Consuls of the last Year. Livy says, there were kill'd 21 Tribunes of War, and 80 of the Senatorial Rank. Paulus having his Horse kill'd, was offered another after the Defeat to escape; but, tho' the Battle was fought against his Advice, he disdained to survive the Loss: He chose to die fighting; while Terentius, whose Rashness was the Cause of it, saved himself by Flight, accompanied only with 70 Horse to Venusia; the Town where Horace 152 Years after was born.

99 Marcus Claudius Marcellus was five times Consul, the first in the Year 532. He was a most excellent General, and the first who gave the Romans an Instance, that Annibal could be beat. It was he who took Syracuse, after a Siege of three Years; the great Mathematician Archimedes having so long defended it by his astonishing Engines.

He was generally successful in what he undertook, and this probably led him to the last Action of his Life, which was too rash: For, in his 5th Consulate, in the 545th Year of Rome, 208 before Christ, being with the Army in Apulia, encamped a few Miles from that of Annibal, he rode out with his Collegue Crispinus, who was also there, and a Guard of 220 Horse, to view a Hill that lay between the two Camps, with a Design to possess and fortify it. But Annibal, who was never wanting for a Contrivance, had placed an Ambush of about 2000 below it. These surrounding the Consuls, and the few that stay'd with them (for most of their Men fled) Marcellus, as he was couragiously defending himself, was run through with a Launce, and died: Crispinus and Marcellus's Son escaped grievously wounded. Annibal on finding his Body, caused it (according to Custom) to be burnt, and sent his Bones and Ashes in a Silver Urn to his Son, as Plutarch says, who has given us his Life; but he quotes Valerius

Maximus and Livy, for what is not to be found in their Books, as we now have them; tho' we have the Passages in both, that mention this Act of Humanity in Annibal, viz. Valerius Maximus, *lib.* 5. *c.* 1. and Livy, *lib.* 27. *c.* 28. for neither of them say anything of sending away the Bones.

100 Instances of this are to be found in Livy, particularly when A. Atilius Calatinus (mention'd in Note 86) in the first Punic War, was leading the Roman Army from Mutistratum in Sicily, which they had most barbarously destroyed, to the Siege of Camarina, they fell in their march into such a disadvantageous Situation, and were so surrounded by the Carthaginian Army, that it appeared impossible for them to avoid either being all taken, or all cut to Pieces, till M. Calpburnius Flamma, a Tribune, with 300 Men, whom he led on with these Words,

> *Come Soldiers, let us march on and die, and*
> *by our Deaths save the rest of the Army,*

took Possession of a Hill, where they alone kept the Enemy so long employ'd, before they could quite vanquish and destroy them, that the main Body found Means to retreat. All the 300, 'tis said, fell there; but Flamma was found with some Life left, and recovered.

Another Instance was, when in the War with the Samnites, P. Decius Mus, one of those who devoted themselves (as in Note 68) to save the Roman Army, acted the same Part, but with better Fortune; for their Enemies were so astonished at the Attempt, that they both let the Army retreat, and these People also escape. The Story is in Livy, *lib.* 7. *c.* 34, &c. and both these Passages are mentioned in Manlius's Speech against redeeming the Roman Captives taken at Cannæ, *Livy, lib.* 22. 60.

## CHAPTER XXI

101 They resided in the South-east Parts of Italy, formerly called Magna Græcia, or Great Greece, now the Kingdom of Naples. The People were from Greece, and spoke that Language.

102 In Plato's Pheadon, now in English from Dacier's French Version.

# *Acknowledgments*

*Gratitude is not only the greatest of virtues,*
*but the parent of all others.*
*– Cicero*

How do you present two towering figures of literature and the ages in a new edition? Carefully, and only after consulting the experts. We are indebted to the author and scholar Ross King and to Harold Augenbraum of the National Book Foundation; they linked us to Victor Shea and William Whitla of York University and to the Franklin biographer Stacy Schiff. We are also grateful to Jack Lynch of Rutgers University and Kevin Berland of the Pennsylvania State University, who led us to James N. Green at the Library Company of Philadelphia.

Our thanks to Robert Greenman and Tom Morris for their research. Special thanks to Professor John Guson for being the first reader, and to Robert Hittel for being the first believer.

# *Uncommon Books for Serious Readers*

**Boston**
Henry Cabot Lodge

**A Boy at the Hogarth Press**
Written and illustrated by
Richard Kennedy

**The Dream**
Sir Winston Churchill

**Feeding the Mind**
Lewis Carroll

**A Fortnight in the Wilderness**
Alexis de Tocqueville

**The Little Guide to Your Well-Read Life**
Steve Leveen

**The Making of The Finest Hour**
Speech by Winston S. Churchill
Introduction by Richard M. Langworth

**New York**
Theodore Roosevelt

**Rare Words**
Jan Leighton
and Hallie Leighton

**Samuel Johnson's Dictionary**
Selections from the 1755 work
that defined the English language
Edited by Jack Lynch

**Samuel Johnson's Insults**
Edited by Jack Lynch

**The Silverado Squatters**
Six selected chapters
Robert Louis Stevenson

**Words That Make a Difference**
Robert Greenman